This book should be the date

BEHIND THE SOFA

BEHIND THE SOFA

CELEBRITY MEMORIES OF
DOCTOR WHO

EDITED BY
STEVE BERRY

FOREWORD BY TERRY PRATCHETT

GOLLANCZ
LONDON

All rights reserved

The right of Steve Berry to be identified as the editor of this work has been
asserted by him in accordance with the
Copyright, Designs and Patents Act 1988.

Illustrations and design concept by Ben Morris
www.benmorrisillustration.com

First published in 2012 by Matador

Expanded edition first published in Great Britain in 2013 by Gollancz
An imprint of the Orion Publishing Group
Orion House, 5 Upper St Martin's Lane, London WC2H 9EA
An Hachette UK Company

A CIP catalogue record for this book is available
from the British Library

ISBN (Cased) 978 0 575 12945 0

1 3 5 7 9 10 8 6 4 2

Printed in Great Britain by CPI Group (UK) Ltd, Croydon CR0 4YY

The Orion Publishing Group's policy is to use papers that are natural,
renewable and recyclable products and made from wood grown in sustainable
forests. The logging and manufacturing processes are expected to conform to
the environmental regulations of the country of origin.

www.alzheimersresearchuk.org
www.benmorrisillustration.com
www.orionbooks.co.uk

In memory of Janet Berry

CONTENTS

Foreword

Rebecca Wood
Chief Executive, Alzheimer's Research UK

A fear of the unknown led Steve Berry to get in touch with us. His late mum, Janet, had been diagnosed with early-onset Alzheimer's — she was still in her 50s. He wanted to know what the future held for her and the family and learn more about this devastating disease and other forms of dementia.

Steve's enthusiasm to help us defeat dementia soon spilled into his life-long passion for Doctor Who. His ambition to publish Behind the Sofa, full of celebrities' memories of their favourite Time Lord, has now become an exciting reality with the aim of raising desperately needed funds for our pioneering dementia research.

Jon Pertwee and Tom Baker were the Doctors of my childhood. I loved the series but it terrified me too. I cowered behind the sofa calling out, "What's happening now?" On reflection, I wonder if this introduction to scientific fantasy inspired my interest in science — I'd like to think it continues to inspire many others.

Royalties from Behind the Sofa are being donated to Alzheimer's Research UK. Everyone who buys a copy will give hope to the hundreds of thousands of people in the UK living with dementia today. The money raised will bring us closer to finding ways to diagnose, prevent, treat and cure dementia — one of the biggest medical challenges of our lifetime.

Behind the Sofa is a lasting legacy to Steve's mum and dementia research. If only we could travel through time like the Time Lords and get a glimpse of what's to come — hopefully it would meet our vision of a world free from dementia.

Preface

Steve Berry
Editor

I don't think my mum ever understood my love of Doctor Who. If pushed, she would probably have had only one strong memory of the show: me, standing at the top of the stairs, crying about how the "jelly men" were going to get me. Yet, even as a terrified six-year-old, I insisted on watching week after week. Slowly but surely, I became a fan. Sorry, Mum, for those sleepless Saturday nights but it was with good reason they called it *Terror of the Zygons*.

Years later, as Russell T Davies magnificently midwifed the series through its 2005 revival, many hitherto undeclared celebrity Whovians also sang its praises in public. At the same time, Alzheimer's was robbing my mum of her memories and I found myself asking, "What would the Doctor do if faced with an enemy like this?"

The answer I arrived at was a seemingly simple one. I would harness all the public goodwill and enthusiasm for Doctor Who to compile a book of famous favourite memories, then sell it and raise lots of money for charity. So began a campaign of letter-writing, string-pulling and Twitter-bombing on my part to persuade as many well-known names as possible to contribute. It took a little longer than expected but, finally, here is the finished article.

I'd like to take this opportunity to thank my wife, Jo. She has not only had to put up with my peculiar celebrity obsession for the past five years, but also the demands of looking after my mum as her Alzheimer's worsened. Sorry, Jo, I don't think you completely understand my love of Doctor Who either but now, hopefully, the following people can help shed some light on it...

Introduction

Sir Terry Pratchett

I was there at the beginning. That's what I remember — watching the first episode twice, because of public demand and that pesky business with the grassy knoll. And I remember the dreadful pepperpots appearing, and the moment that the first companions — that strange grandchild and those remarkable and rare teachers who took everything in their stride, including time travel and a police box bigger on the inside — left, and we realised that in the so-far surprisingly safe world of Doctor Who things could change. They were barely mentioned again, as far as I remember. And the series marched on. Until the great defining moment, the decision that would propel the series on for 50 years — the change of the main character, the first regeneration. It's easy to forget now how groundbreaking that moment was. Our hero dies — and the series continues, a different lead with different tics but somehow still the same man.

I wasn't that bothered at the time, not really. I was 18 when Patrick Troughton took over from William Hartnell and other things — mad, confusing, exciting things like drink, girls, Daleks — no wait, not those — were happening. But I still watched it when I could, and some of those moments are still with me. It's funny that way, Doctor Who — it's been such a part of the DNA of Great Britain for so many years now that even if you didn't watch it religiously, you probably know more about it than you think. Daleks, Cybermen, bigger on the inside — everyone knows what you're talking about. And it was always a safe option for Saturday afternoon tea with the family. Doctors came and went, but for 26 years it was part of this country's shared heritage and memory. Anybody my age or younger has been informed by it, moulded by it, at least to some degree. For so many during those years it was their first introduction to Science Fiction (nevertheless, when people talk about Doctor Who, I recall the science fiction before Doctor Who, when Gollancz championed real international science fiction writers. Bliss was it in that dawn to be alive. I was there at the dawn of real science fiction. No screwdrivers allowed) and its influence is far-reaching. Generations of authors, screenwriters, actors, dreamers found their escape in the wonky corridors and Styrofoam monsters of this enduring institution.

And then it went away. It wasn't the end of the world, as far as I was concerned — I had watched a few episodes with my daughter, but it wasn't for me anymore, and at times was obviously suffering from lack of budget and care from the BBC. I was saddened for the kids who would grow up without that comforting madness in their lives, telling them that you could be good and clever and save the day and you didn't have to brandish a gun to achieve those things. But the wheel turns and all things shall come to pass (after an entertaining but ridiculously American stutter with Paul McGann) and there it was, back on Saturday nights, the odd bloke with the phone box that travels in time, having adventures and saving the day.

And I watched it, and it was great. It reminded me of my childhood, which is always a nice thing at my age. But, at last, we had a Doctor who could act — and I mean could really act. Oh, it wasn't science fiction any more — had it ever really been? — there was too much waving of screwdrivers and flying of spaceships looking like The Titanic and "the day has been saved because". Not because of anything that made sense, quite often, just because. That's not SF, not really — that's make-it-up-as-you-go-alongium. But that's okay, as the show has never really pretended to be much more. And the recent actors have been wonderful, drawing that line back to the grumpy old man who kicked it all off 50 years ago. And the Daleks are still scary, which isn't something you can say about many half-century-old alien designs. I've enjoyed some episodes of it more than others, and that's fine as well, because hey, that's life. But I love the fact that there are children out there who are learning that life can take you anywhere, and anything can happen, and it can be fantastic. But also that sometimes, life takes away as well. The hero can fail, or die, and we don't all have a magical hand-wavey way to regenerate ourselves. It's an important lesson.

I've worked very closely with Alzheimer's Research UK since my diagnosis with this terrible, horrible disease, and know first-hand how important their work is. I'm glad to have been asked to write this introduction, bringing together some of the warmest memories of my childhood and some of the most important work being done to stem Alzheimer's. Thank you for buying this book — the royalties will go towards vital research. But I hope you enjoy it, as well. Your memories won't always tally with everything here, but then two peoples' memories never do exactly match. They're personal, and define the personality, in a way which we can barely grasp. If we ever reach that level of understanding, then perhaps we'll be on the way to some sort of cure. Real life doesn't have sonic screwdrivers or handy time machines or 900-year-old geniuses to save the day. All it has is hard work, careful experimentation and, above all, hope that things can be better. In the end, perhaps that is the best lesson Doctor Who can teach us — things can be better, and hope is always worthwhile.

And perhaps that strangers sometimes are to be trusted.

Terry Pratchett
Salisbury, UK

Chris Tarrant

Radio and TV presenter
Advertised the Doctor's favourite sweets, jelly babies, on TV in 1979

When I was growing up, the bit I loved was when the Daleks said, "Exterminate!" — they were the only real baddies I remember. I loved all that! That was good, at the time, but the rest of it got a bit silly. I suppose, years later, when my old mate Sylvester McCoy became Doctor Who, I thought, "Hey, a friend of mine is the Doctor, that's kind of cool."

Sylvester is one of the daftest men you'll meet — a very funny man. He used to do a wonderful werewolf routine on Tiswas which was quite extraordinary. We stayed once in a hotel down in the Wye Valley — we were going to be filming there — and for some reason, Sylv got down there before us. He was one of those people; if you left him with time on his hands, he'd get bored and he used to do stupid things.

So we'd arrived, and the manager said, "Mr Tarrant, can we have a word?" and I said, "Yes, of course, what's up?" He said, "Er, Mr McCoy's here and he's causing a bit of a problem in the car parking area."

"Don't eat the fish, whatever you do!"

Apparently — and I don't for the life of me know why — he'd been sitting around waiting for us by the front window of this great big, grand hotel with wonderful grounds and, while the people were arriving for their early evening dinner, parking up their Bentleys and Mercedes and so on, Sylv had hurled himself backwards out into the rhododendrons.

He has this amazing India rubber body, so he was rolling around between the parking cars, grabbing himself around the throat, choking and screaming, "Don't eat the fish, whatever you do! Don't eat the fish!"

So all these people arriving for their meal are suddenly saying, "I don't think the halibut's for me, thank you." You have to think: what sort of a brain comes up with that? Bloody Sylv! That's who.

Ian McMillan
Poet, playwright and broadcaster
Namechecked Doctor Who (and Match Of The Day!) in a poem commissioned for the UK's digital TV switchover

I was always a big fan of Doctor Who as a lad (I was born in 1956) and I can vividly remember watching the first episode at my auntie's down North Street; I enjoyed the oddness of it, the weirdness of it, and the fact that they were travelling through time which, in the early 1960s, felt like a scientific breakthrough that was just round the corner. I even remember the name of the school that was featured in the episode: Coal Hill School — and, no, I've not looked it up on the internet!

"I remember being disappointed when they landed."

I realise that I could look up all sorts of Doctor Who-related things online, but I prefer my actual memories, hazy as they might be.

So one of my favourite episodes comes from quite early on in the first series, I think, and it's about the TARDIS being trapped somewhere in time and space (how those words resonated to an eight-year-old!) and at least one episode was just the Doctor and his assistants whirling through nothingness. I'm sure that episode (and maybe there was more than one) was the beginning of an appreciation of off-centre stories, of surrealism and Dadaism, of the macabre and the uncanny.

I remember being disappointed when they landed somewhere; I wanted them to fly round in the middle of nowhere for ever!

[Editor's note: Ian is most likely remembering 1964's two-parter The Edge Of Destruction/The Brink Of Disaster, set entirely within the TARDIS and featuring a visual effect of a melting ormolu clock.]

Tony Lee
Writer and comic book author
Aged 10, created a hand-typed and photocopied fanzine called K-9

The first time I wrote the words "Time Lord" professionally, I had to take a break. I sat back, smiled, and remembered exactly what those words meant to me.

You see, all my childhood I wanted to be a Time Lord. I wanted to travel in time and space and fight Daleks and the Master and do all that cool stuff I saw the Doctor doing every week. Doctor Who was much better than Star Trek, or Star Wars — an argument that caused much dissension in the playground — but I didn't care. Unfortunately, as I grew up, my formative teenage years had no Doctor. He was on hiatus or, dare I say it — cancelled. But I never gave up. Even after the McGann wilderness years I soldiered on, in time writing for TV, radio, comics — and waiting for the chance when I could write the Doctor's stories for real.

I pitched my first Doctor Who comic a week before it was announced that Christopher Eccleston would be returning. I got my first greenlit script (for Doctor Who Magazine) the month after David Tennant took over as the Tenth Doctor. And I remember the joy I had when I got the job — the sheer, fanboy glee. I wished more than anything that I was that Time Lord, that I could get into my TARDIS and travel back to the early 1980s, find that skinny little boy that always hung out in the park in Hayes and tell him, "You know what you do? You get to write what the Doctor says when you grow up."

"All my childhood I wanted to be a Time Lord."

Since that day I've written several more Doctor Who comics, including one with all 10 Doctors. But none of them equal that first, wonderful moment when I wrote the words "Time Lord" professionally.

Josie Long
Comedian
Went on the TUC's anti-cuts march in 2011 accompanied by a Dalek

Basically, for me, there are three really, really great things about Doctor Who.

The first one is how I got my little brother into it…

When it came back, with Christopher Eccleston, my little brother was maybe seven. And, because he's my half-brother and I've never lived with him, we used to ring each other every single week before and after Doctor Who and I would talk to him about how excited he was and how excited I was. And afterwards we would have a very serious appraisal of the episode and what had happened in it, and whether or not we thought the monsters were good, and whether or not we thought the Doctor was good, and what we thought of the companion. It was brilliant.

The second one is my friend, Daniel, who is a lifetime Doctor Who lover…

He's a year younger than me but he's properly seen everything, read everything, listened to everything. And, because we used to live together, we'd have Doctor Who parties and it was just delightful. Completely delightful.

Here's how to have a Doctor Who party:

You watch Doctor Who and you get really, really over-excited about it. Then, afterwards, you watch Doctor Who Confidential and then you go on the message boards and get really annoyed by the people responding to the episode. Then you try to calm Daniel down, and you cook him dinner. And sometimes your friend Tom comes over who's really, really big into Doctor Who and then Tom and Dan have, like, three-hour long discussions/arguments.

And the third one is *The Greatest Show in the Galaxy*…

Now, its official title may be *The Greatest Show in the Galaxy*, but I always call it The Circus of Death. Every time: The Circus of Death. Sylvester McCoy is my hero. There's no shame in that; he was a properly trained clown, that man.

So, in The Circus of Death there were a family of monsters, the Gods of Ragnarok, and they would demand you perform for them, and then kill you if you didn't satisfy them. I think, because I was a young precocious child, the idea of people killing you if you weren't good enough for performing was, to me, more chilling than Freddy Krueger. It was absolutely the most terrifying thing I saw as a child. And, I have to add, when I was growing up, I wasn't allowed to watch any films with sex scenes, because my parents were quite religious, but I was allowed to watch loads of 18 rated horror films. The Circus of Death was scarier than any 18 rated horror films.

> **"Sylvester McCoy is my hero. There's no shame in that."**

Toyah Willcox
Singer and actress
Had a top 10 hit written by the man behind Who-fan band, Blood Donor

Haven't we all hidden behind the sofa when Doctor Who was on the telly?

I've been alive a lot longer than most and consider myself lucky enough to have seen the original Doctor, William Hartnell, who personified the iconic father figure while being terrifyingly mysterious. Hartnell has never been equalled for me because he was the oldest of all the Doctors and his silvery age added weight to making me believe his power.

That said, when Doctor Who was made into a cinema film in 1965, as Dr Who and the Daleks with Peter Cushing as the Doctor, I still insisted on going. The problem with seeing a horror film in public when you are only seven years old is that it's unforgivable to show fear. Even the opening sequences of mist-covered marsh lands surrounding the Daleks' city had me frozen to the spot. I remember wanting to slide down the seat and hide but I was flanked by my parents who were all too ready to laugh at my fear. So I sat, wide-eyed and as petrified as those on-screen forests, for two tortuous and exhilarating hours... which kept me in full supply of nightmares for a good month.

> **"I sat, wide-eyed and as petrified as those on-screen forests."**

Luckily, by the time the Cybermen appeared on the TV screens I was approaching the age of the "ratty pubescent teen", and started to find the whole concept of Doctor Who highly erotic.

And I still do!

Gareth Roberts

Screenwriter and novelist
Was nicknamed Scaroth Roberts for the duration of October 1979

For the first 23 years of my life, I had a strange suspicion that I was missing out on something. The trouble being, I didn't know what that something was. My contemporaries seemed always to be getting very excited about things that, while fine in themselves, stirred little reaction in me — passing their driving test, going outside, or the Thompson Twins, for example.

Then, suddenly and terribly, I discovered that missing link in the last place and among the last people I would ever have expected.

I was in my final year of college and I met a student called Steve.

Steve had heard a dirty rumour that I was writing a Doctor Who novel, and so he invited me to a pub in London where, once a month, he and his Doctor Who fan friends met for a drink.

My previous experiences of fellow fans had not been good ones. At the age of 11 I'd joined the Doctor Who Appreciation Society in the mistaken belief that it was a society for the appreciation of Doctor Who. Their newsletters disproved this spectacularly. They were utterly baffling, full of Daily Mail-esque rants about jokes in the series (in their opinion, *there should be no jokes*), and articles incandescent with rage about people I'd never heard of.

I was just as frightened of the few fans that had crossed my path — the Tory boy who pronounced *Logopolis* differently every time he said it (which was often) and another lad who never took his coat off and returned my copy of Doctor Who and the Doomsday Weapon with a curious stain on page 81.

So, as Steve led me into the pub, I was wary. Then he introduced me to his friends. And I started talking to them. And they started talking to me. Some of them had names I recognised from Doctor Who Magazine and other fanzines (oh yes, I'd lurked on the sidelines, but I didn't inhale). We talked a lot about *The Underwater Menace* that night, I'm sure, but we also talked about Bowie, Twin Peaks, Hartley Hare, the European Union, sex and Quentin Crisp.

"Somewhere there are people who will laugh at your impression of Queen Katryca."

An hour later I finally knew what I'd been missing. Because these people should have been my friends way before. In my teens I should have been with them, laughing and drinking and learning and, quite frankly, feeling some of them up. They'd grown up, gay alongside straight, boy alongside girl, nerd alongside jock, in a way I had never conceived was possible. And the thing that drew them together, and drew me to them, and supplied the missing something in my life, was Doctor Who.

The moral of this story is that somewhere out there are people who will laugh at, and love you for, your impression of Queen Katryca trying to navigate the corridors of Marb Station. They're waiting for you. Go out and find them.

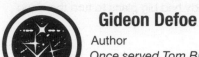

Gideon Defoe

Author

Once served Tom Baker a pint of Guinness at The Coal Hole pub on The Strand

In the early 1980s we moved house.

My mum carefully explained that this new place was rented, which meant it belonged to someone else, which meant we had to take good care of it. I figured it was incredibly nice of some stranger to let us borrow an entire house, so I should probably do more than just *take care of it*: I should try to *improve* it.

I resolved to accomplish this via a radical makeover of my bedroom. It was a pretty small room, so an obvious priority was to make it look more spacious.

You know what else was small yet seemed spacious? The TARDIS. I didn't think this was entirely down to multi-dimensional Time Lord engineering — no, I thought it was at least partly due to clever interior design choices. Namely: roundels.

Like a pint-sized, slightly less dickish Laurence Llewelyn-Bowen I found the most heavy-duty felt-tip pen I could and proceeded

"I drew a video screen listing the TARDIS occupants."

to draw around a dinner plate until the wall, or at least the amount of wall a six-year-old could reach standing on his bed, was covered with beautiful, vaguely wonky Davison-era roundels. As a finishing flourish, I also drew a video screen listing the TARDIS occupants: the Doctor, lovely Nyssa, gobby Tegan and Adric. Then I crossed out Adric, adding a slightly cold "deceased", and put my own name in there instead.

When I dragged my mum in to see my handiwork, with a proud explanatory shout of "roundels!" she was so impressed that she went the exact same colour as the big rubber snake in *Kinda*. I generously offered to continue my makeover throughout the rest of the house but she seemed to be too busy crying and saying things like "lost deposit" and "should have had it adopted" to listen.

Which was a pity, because I already had big plans to turn the airing cupboard into a Zero Cabinet.

 ## Javier Grillo-Marxuach

Television screenwriter and producer
Spent a day dressed as the Master at a Doctor Who convention in 2010

In the late 1970s, during the Star Wars boom, television programmers scrambled to get as much sci-fi on the air as possible. In my native homeland of Puerto Rico (which, by the way, I still believe to have been the inspiration for Porto Guava in Gerry Anderson's Joe 90), this meant that Doctor Who aired on weeknights under the title El Doctor Misterio.

And so, every night I would watch a logo which clearly read "Doctor Who" vanish into a maelstrom and wonder why the Spanish-language voice-over was announcing a significantly different title than the one I was reading.

> **"Unfashionably middle-aged, manifestly googly-eyed, viciously eccentric."**

Translational disconnects aside, I would be remiss if I didn't faithfully report that at the age of eight I found the good Doctor's adventures profoundly… well… weird. Weirdly dubbed, weirdly shifting between film and videotape in a style defiantly not resembling the mainstream TV production methods of our North American pop-cultural overlords, and weirdly located in a country whose climate and texture bore little resemblance to the tropical environment in which I was raised.

There was also the Doctor himself, unfashionably middle-aged, manifestly googly-eyed, viciously eccentric: he was the epitome of everything this child of the Han Solo generation was taught to find weird in a hero.

Thankfully, weird was always my favorite colour.

And so, in spite of the protestations of my friends — who believed that this weird show had little currency with the space opera we loved

on the big screen — I became a young, non-anglophone Whovian…
and spent many a restless night wondering where in a tropical
paradise one could purchase a twelve-foot-long woollen scarf.

Though my dreams of owning Tom Baker's outfit would not come
true until much later in life — and in a climate far more welcoming
to the garments — my childhood viewing of El Doctor Misterio
was the gateway drug to Blake's 7, The Hitchhiker's Guide to the
Galaxy, The Prisoner, and every other British science fiction series
I might have missed had the Doctor not encouraged me to further
embrace the less-than-familiar…

And sometimes, to this day, on occasion, when I happen to buy
a bag of jelly babies, I will hold it out to a stranger and ask "¿Le
gustaria una gomita?"

Michael Moorcock

Author
*Wrote an Eleventh Doctor novel, The Coming of the
Terraphiles, in 2009*

I remember reading in the Radio Times about Doctor Who
coming. It sounded a bit more interesting than most programmes
of the day so at the appropriate time we fired up the old steam
viewer and sat down to watch.

I was a bit disappointed with William Hartnell, who played everything
at full volume and was pretty stilted in his delivery, exactly as he was
in The Army Game. But, by the time Patrick Troughton turned up
to give the character his trademark fey
eccentricities, I was hooked.

**"We fired up the old
steam viewer and sat
down to watch."**

For me, the best 20th century Doctor
Who was Tom Baker, whose reign
lasted until it no longer became possible
for me to watch regularly. I remained
unimpressed by 2001: A Space Odyssey, but I'd go to considerable
lengths not to miss an episode of *The Brain of Morbius*.

It wasn't until Christopher Eccleston arrived that I had a chance
to watch regularly again and, I have to say, I became a bit of an

addict. The plots became increasingly complex, playing with ideas of time and space, and the actors more suited to a role that blended comedy and melodrama.

Because I now watch on Public Service Broadcasting in the USA, I'm usually a season or two behind, which can be frustrating...

Especially when you're trying to write a novel about a Doctor Who you haven't actually seen yet!

Michelle Duncan

Actress
Was understudied at her Doctor Who read-through by David Tennant's mum

For me, a gangly child in a village in Scotland, there was nothing cuddly or nostalgic about Doctor Who, even if my memory makes it so now. From the discordant harmonies of the theme tune to the shrill hypertension of the Daleks' voice, this was for me genuine science fiction; dark, transgressive, and vividly imaginative. The alien civilisations seemed claustrophobic and at times, palpably evil. The relationships between the Doctor and his assistants seemed exotic in their very sexlessness.

I think I have a dim vestigial memory of Tom Baker — could I be retconning? — but it was his immediate followers who were to me the real, er, McCoy: I was mesmerised by his transmogrifications, and the pleasing fact that this Time Lord, with all of space-time as his domain, had a predilection not just for our random "planet number three from the sun", but actually for Britain...

"I had no idea how terrifying the real werewolf would be."

Which brings me to 19th century Scotland; or, in reality, to 21st century Wales, where I played Lady Isobel MacLeish of the Torchwood Estate in *Tooth and Claw*. Much of acting is just that — acting — but being heavily chained in a darkened basement, with the terrifying Tom Smith as the Host making blood-curdling cries of anguish, there was little need for pretence. My most vivid memory is of hiding beside a long Victorian wooden kitchen table, clutching at my maids, all of us staring at an excessively tall man in a leotard with a tennis ball stuck on the end of a pole to give us an eye-line to the werewolf terrorising Torchwood. At the time, I had no idea how terrifying the real werewolf would turn out to be, but luckily a man in a leotard was just the right amount of scary.

In one particular take, my heel broke during an escape, giving me a sudden authentic look of horror as I contemplated a tumble down some Medieval flagstones. Much as I loved the episode, I wasn't prepared to give my life for it, so I clutched at Billie Piper's clothes in a lunging attempt to stay upright. In retrospect, I wonder what it would have been like to be a Doctor Who martyr — at least it would have made my character's collector card more collectable.

Other long-running TV series can become "institutions" — that deadening, heavy word. Doctor Who mixes a peculiarly British improvisational joy into the legacy of the past. Great characters — Sherlock Holmes, James Bond — give you the impression that they existed long before their creators stumbled upon them. The Doctor is in that league. Raise your glass, then, to Sydney Newman and Verity Lambert, for having the serendipity to discover this great, intense, eccentric character who'd been knocking around Gallifrey for nine hundred years.

Nicholas Briggs

Actor, writer, director and voice of many Doctor Who monsters
Taught Prince Charles how to speak like a Dalek

When I first went to drama school, one of our tasks was to tell a story to the group and they had to work out whether we were telling the truth or not. I told them that Doctor Who had saved my life. The story went like this…

"Doctor Who saved my life."

When I was a kid, I was told I "had to go" to Sea Scout camp; but I refused to, because it would mean missing the final part of *Planet of the Daleks*. Resisting much pressure and a fair deal of humiliation, I stayed at home and, naturally, thoroughly enjoyed that episode.

That night, however, I woke up and was terribly ill, vomiting and passing out, and was rescued from choking by my parents. If that'd happened at Scout camp, I might well have wandered off into the bushes on my own, feeling sick, and I might have ended up choking while unconscious. Hence my slightly over-dramatic assertion to my fellow students that Doctor Who had saved me.

Everyone in the group thought the story was preposterous and that I'd made it up. I'm not sure what exactly the exercise proved, but it certainly made it clear to everyone in my year at drama school, from the outset, that I was a complete and utter Doctor Who nut.

Richard Madeley

Columnist, novelist, television and radio presenter
Corrected Paul Merton's allegation that Daleks can't "go upstairs" on an episode of Have I Got News For You

I'm just old enough — let me emphasise the "just", thank you — yes, *just* old enough to remember my very first episode of Doctor Who, partly because *it* was the first episode of Doctor Who... or rather, the first two episodes of Doctor Who.

Let me explain.

The opening programme was repeated, in its entirety, the following Saturday. It was November, 1963. Two for the price of one. Why?

Kennedy. The assassination of the US president in Dallas, Texas, barely a day before the first scheduled transmission of the BBC's hugely-anticipated new series. I was seven and a half; my sister Elizabeth was 11. We couldn't wait for the first Doctor Who.

But Kennedy's assassination shrouded everything. Viewers were utterly preoccupied by the extraordinary, horrible news event and the BBC felt, as the following week unfolded, that the big launch of their intriguing fantasy drama had been eclipsed by brutal reality. So they decided, perfectly understandably, to launch it again.

I'm not sure, but I think that on the subsequent Saturday they tacked episode two onto the back of episode one. I seem to recall a double treat. (You'll have to check.)

But anyway, William Hartnell's Doctor and his granddaughter, Susan, the first of many such pairings, are burned into my memory, as is the first glimpse of the impossibly vast expanse of the interior of the tiny box-like TARDIS. We're perfectly used to it now, but I can't tell you how much that initial experience of the *physically impossible* brought with it the shock of the new. It was a brilliant conceptual stroke and secured the watching audience's attention from the off.

I was never frightened by Doctor Who. I never hid behind the sofa, never pulled a Dralon cushion in front of my eyes. I did once have a nightmare about a Cyberman, but that's about it. I think this is because, for me, the birth of this extraordinary TV phenomenon will always be inextricably linked to Kennedy's assassination. I remember the first newsflash that brought us that news at 7pm in the evening and my shocked parents' instant tears of overwhelmed grief. I'd never seen them cry before.

> **"The Doctor and his granddaughter are burned into my memory."**

Maybe that's why, for all its skill, guile and shock value, Doctor Who could never quite match the reality of the horror and pathos of a young president's awful end.

Richard Marson

Former Blue Peter series editor
Wrote JN-T: The Life and Scandalous Times of John Nathan-Turner, a biography of Doctor Who's most controversial former producer

"Wait here…"

We were shown into a large featureless room, with drab utility furniture and, for a few nerve-wracking minutes, left to our own devices. The summer of 1984 was hot and the room was stuffy. From its windows, a dreary panorama of industrial West London stretched into the distance.

I was here at the BBC's North Acton rehearsal rooms with my best friend, Patrick Mulkern, to interview Patrick Troughton and Frazer

Hines, guest stars of the story then in production, *The Two Doctors*. Troughton was notoriously publicity shy and rumoured to be tricky, so I was both thrilled and daunted when JN-T said he'd persuaded the actor to talk to me for Doctor Who Monthly. By now, I was used to interviewing all kinds of people from the show but this promised to be an out of the ordinary encounter. It was meant to be a solo assignment but, nervous, I wanted back-up and, knowing how Patrick adored Troughton's Doctor, asked him along.

For years afterwards, we often joked about the encounter that followed. How Troughton had seemed somewhat irascible, not bothering to conceal his bemusement at our curiosity and the detail of some of the questions. "But you weren't even born when I was doing it..." he protested at one point. There was a sticky moment when I asked him about his son David's appearance in *The War Games*. Troughton looked blank and flatly denied it. Artlessly, I stood my ground, when I should just have let it go. Sometimes, mid-answer, he would drift off into his own thoughts and run out of steam. Once he pronounced, with sudden import, "The future is in the past!" This became a catchphrase between Patrick and me and always made us laugh. We had our photograph taken with him and then Frazer Hines, who was, by comparison, uncomplicated and super-friendly.

"Troughton was publicity shy and rumoured to be tricky."

Recently, we both had cause to listen to the recording again and compare notes. Leaving aside the usual cringing when confronted with your juvenile self in gauche full flow, we were both struck with how much gentler Troughton seemed. Where was the grumpiness I had so vividly recalled? (JN-T might suggest, "The memory cheats...") The bemusement was still evident but we could better appreciate this. He had almost certainly expected to meet a proper journalist and photographer. Instead, he was faced with two star-struck teenagers grilling him on the details of a job decades past and asking for a few snaps by which to remember the occasion. How sweet of him to sit in that sweltering green room and give us his attention.

And now, bizarrely, that phrase of his I'd mocked so much over the years seems to make sense at last: "The future is in the past..."

Alastair Reynolds
Novelist
Once refused to visit a boy's house in fear of his Dalek wallpaper

My theory is that your favorite Doctor is always going to be the one on television when you're eight, which nicely (and conveniently) squares with my particular enthusiasm for the Pertwee era.

I have precisely no memory of the earlier Doctors, and no strong recollection of the first Pertwee season. Things only begin to come into very hazy focus with the second run of adventures (*Colony in Space* in particular) but even then it's all very fragmented and I wonder how many of the stories I actually saw in their entirety. The Peladon stories have always been rather clear in my memory, for instance, but I have no recollection of catching *The Sea Devils* until rather later in the 1970s.

However poor my memories, though, what is clear is that I fell in love with the series unreservedly. I'd already developed a weird and abiding fascination with the idea of time travel, having been exposed to George Pal's The Time Machine at a very early age. Doctor Who was more of the same, but better! Of course there was not a great deal of time travel (or, indeed, travel) in

> **"I'd already developed a weird and abiding fascination with the idea of time travel."**

those earlier Pertwee days but I think the notion was always there in the background. More importantly, school friends knew a lot more about Doctor Who than I did. I remember being told about the "Cybermen" being the best monsters. Who were these mysterious Cybermen? Jon Pertwee never encountered them, but I suppose the older brothers and sisters of friends would have had recollections of the Troughton era. To them, these earlier monsters would still have been relatively fresh in the memory and preserved as such through the medium of TV annuals, Doctor Who chocolate bars, wallpaper and so on.

I don't think you can overstate the importance of peer influence during those pre-digital, pre-repeat days. When Tom Baker eventually encountered the Cyberleader on Nerva Beacon in *Revenge of the Cybermen*, they had gained (to my nine-year-old eyes) an almost mythic stature. And I thought they were fantastic! I loved the Baker era too, in fact, although because I grew up with it (I was into my teens when it ended) I had inevitably become more questioning and critical over time.

No such difficulties with the Pertwee period. It was wonderfully terrifying but also wonderfully comforting and welcoming. Even now, 40 years on, I can't think of sausage and mash without being transported back to a particular Saturday evening, and *Invasion of the Dinosaurs*. Marvellous!

Alexei Sayle

Comedian, writer and sometime actor
Played the DJ in Revelation of the Daleks

In 1984, I got it into my head that I'd make a good Doctor Who. I wrote a piece for Foundation, a science fiction review magazine, called "Why I Should Have Been the New Doctor Who: The Case for a Marxist in the TARDIS". It may be a kids' TV show, but it always had a lot of political undercurrents, rather like those serials of the 1950s. A lot of the writers had been fleeing the McCarthy trials in the 'States, so you'd often find a perverse communist message in Robin Hood or Lancelot.

Partly in playfulness but partly serious, I set about putting it around that I'd like to be the Doctor. I asked my relatives to post letters from various parts of the country suggesting I could be, and I think I got into The Sun. It was kind of a joke really. But it probably led to me being cast in a story. I didn't have to audition or do any of the usual casting palaver, you know. They just offered a part to me.

Now, I'm not particularly a fan of watching myself on telly but some people really think it was a high-point for Doctor Who. I mean, Colin Baker wasn't a bad Doctor by any means, and his sidekick, Nicola Bryant, was gorgeous. I never got to meet the Doctor on screen — I got zapped too soon — but Colin was always around in rehearsals. It was quite a nice thing to be the last person to be killed by a Dalek for many years.

The funny thing was, when David Tennant first came down to London, he was lodging with a friend of mine, Arabella Weir. And so the first time he met me his hands were shaking because I'd been in Doctor Who. He was always a mad fan. How the tables have turned.

"It was quite nice to be the last person killed by a Dalek."

But it wasn't the greatest period for the series when I did it. Some people thought those hour-long episodes weren't right for the show. The producer, John Nathan-Turner, had built a kind of empire, and the BBC doesn't like that sort of separation, with him being so powerful. So they used that typical politician's trick, to keep cutting the money back year on year, and then said, "Oh, it doesn't look as good as it used to."

There's a sketch I wrote with David Renwick and Andrew Marshall for my show, Stuff, in which a bloke goes to a party and all the other guests are Triffids. We actually wrote it with Daleks in mind — we wanted Daleks — but whoever owned the copyright at the time wouldn't lend them out. By way of revenge, we wrote another sketch about a casting session for the Daleks which didn't feature Daleks at all. We had a guy dressed as a postbox, an Anglepoise lamp, and a sparkler on three cotton reels. They might have killed me on Doctor Who, but I got my own back in the end.

Andrew Cartmel

Former script editor of Doctor Who
Always loved the Doctor Who theme music by Ron Grainer, most especially in the original, eerie, arrangement by Delia Derbyshire

I liked Doctor Who very much but I was never an obsessive fan of it. When I was at university I didn't watch it. I was aware of it, more as a cultural icon in the background. It was thanks to my agent that I was put up for the job of script editor, and got it.

We were being broadcast against Coronation Street, then the most popular show on television, which was widely regarded as the suicide slot. When I moved into the office, which my predecessor had departed in a dramatic fashion, I discovered that I couldn't get into the desk drawer because the key had been snapped off. So we called the BBC carpenter to open it, and inside we found a solitary glass with a red wine stain on it, rolling around forlornly.

So that's what I inherited. There was also one page of a *Tenko* script floating around (about leprosy, I seem to recall) and very much a feeling of "the last days in the bunker". I suppose at least there weren't any cyanide tablets. But the producer, John Nathan-Turner, gave us a free hand: myself, the writers I hired, Sylvester McCoy and Sophie Aldred. I knew early on what we needed to do but it was like getting a ship off the rocks. It took time.

I really felt we'd begun to get good by the time we were doing *Remembrance of the Daleks*. It's such a great script, by Ben Aaronovitch: my favourite line of *Doctor Who* ever is "unlimited rice pudding". Later, when they gave Sylvester a new costume, a darker coat, I remember thinking, "Yes, this is an outward reflection of the inner change". It sounds like a small thing but I thought it was quite symbolically telling.

Foolishly, I didn't actually script any episodes myself. I felt a certain responsibility to encourage new talent and also I didn't know that my window of opportunity was going to be as brief as it was, otherwise I would certainly have written more. However, I did get the chance to pen a couple of memorable speeches. I wrote the "crazy paving" speech, which we dropped into Ian Briggs' script for *Dragonfire*, and I was very pleased to do the final monologue as seen in Rona Munro's *Survival*, the final story of our last series (she wasn't quite so delighted!). I felt at least felt I was allowed to write a eulogy for the show or some kind of farewell message. I'm very proud of that.

> "At least I was allowed to write a eulogy for the show."

Ben, Marc Platt and I had been working together on what eventually became known among fans as The Cartmel Masterplan. (I think it's fair that it was named after me, since the basic impulse to make the Doctor more mysterious and formidable came from me, and also because I discovered and employed those two writers — you might say they were part of *my* masterplan!) It was our thoughts and ideas for the future direction of Doctor Who before we learned it had been formally cancelled in 1989. I like to think that someone might one day stumble across an imaginary envelope containing the details of this plan, in an otherwise empty drawer in our vacated office, perhaps marked "Open in case of emergency"...

Gareth Jenkins

Charity campaigns director
One-time companion of the Doctor in A Fix with Sontarans

So I was the very lucky eight-year-old boy who was chosen to have my dream of meeting the Doctor granted by the now infamous Jimmy Savile.

My overriding memory is of being pretty scared. The whole experience was totally overwhelming. I was fully aware of how many people were going to be watching on television. I'd been in proper rehearsals with the lovely Colin Baker and Janet Fielding in the days before the studio recording. My scrapbook for autographs was packed with the signatures and kind messages of dozens of BBC stars I'd met, including plenty from Grange Hill and Eastenders.

"The Doctor has been my own personal Jesus."

I was so nervous. The night before the recording, my mum, dad, very excited little sister and I were being driven to our hotel in a black taxi, chaperoned by our TV producer, Jeremy Geelan. Unfortunately for him he was sitting opposite me in the back of the cab — I say "unfortunately" because I proceeded to projectile vomit all over him. We had to stop off and hose out the cab at a petrol station. I was still feeling pretty sick with fear the next day, hence my deathly pallor on screen.

But it was wonderful. I had all my family with me, including my incredibly proud Italian grandmother — a seamstress in the war — who had painstakingly created my Doctor Who replica outfit. It was the best Christmas present I ever had as a kid. Or maybe ever. And my favourite cousins were there too, with my younger sister, on the famous bean bags in the opening section of the programme where Savile introduced that week's line-up sitting among the kids. Sadly, a chilling image now. Suffice to say nothing happened to me. He was merely stand-offish and self-centred, only becoming animated when the cameras were rolling.

It might sound trite to say that the experience was life-changing but it actually has been. The Doctor has been my own personal Jesus, encouraging me to do something good with my life. In 2001, the year the Jim'll Fix It script foretold I'd be defending the Earth from Sontaran attack, I was working in advertising. It didn't feel right. It wasn't what the Doctor would have done. Two years later I'd switched to the charity sector, and now I run global campaigns to protect children in war zones for Save the Children. I know that in great part I've got the Doctor, and the BBC, to thank for doing what I am today.

Jamie Anderson

Son of Gerry Anderson and director of Anderson Entertainment
Has a video of himself in a Dalek singing the theme from Fireball XL5 through a ring modulator

My love for Doctor Who was once described by my father — on screen, no less — as "the real tragedy of my life". We were being interviewed for a celebratory documentary called 30 Years in the TARDIS, released on video in 1993. By that stage I was already long hooked, having four years previously been handed a VHS of a Jon Pertwee story somehow mislabelled "The Day of Daleks".

"How could that story get anyone hooked?"

(I know what you're thinking! How could that story get anyone hooked? Actually, at the age of four I thought that the story was great. I was gripped from the opening titles. Even with the disappointing Dalek "army" that materialised in the final episode, I still loved every minute.)

Then, thanks to that one off-hand quote, everyone got wind of the fact that Mr Thunderbirds' son preferred Doctor Who to his own father's Supermarionation series. For Dad I think that meant mild dismay, but for a young boy it meant amazing awesomeness!

Through the 1990s, thanks to a resurgence in popularity of Thunderbirds on TV, I found myself in the enviable position of being able to meet a few of the Doctors, along with the occasional lovely assistant: Sylvester McCoy and (the very cool) Sophie Aldred on a Sunday morning show called Parallel 9; Peter Davison, walking around Henley; Jon Pertwee (very briefly) at an airport. But the ultimate culmination of these incredible few years was meeting my namesake (and favourite) companion, Jamie McCrimmon (AKA Frazer Hines) on the set of the documentary. In my pre-adolescent mind, we even flew the TARDIS together! (In fact, I think we shared just a few moments, mostly of me standing nervously near a recreation of the ship's console. But it felt amazing.)

I still have a small selection of Dalek and TARDIS toys (mostly the old Dapol figures) on my desk at home, and I even enjoy the new series too from time to time. I'm also finally the proud owner of a restored DVD edition of *Day of the Daleks*, with its bigger Dalek invasion force and all-new special effects — I enjoyed watching it more than ever! Looking back, wasn't I lucky that Dad was so tolerant of my love of Doctor Who despite the obvious embarrassment it caused him?

Cheers, Dad!

Jessica Martin

Actress and graphic novelist
Played Mags in The Greatest Show in the Galaxy, *and voiced the Queen in* Voyage of the Damned

At the time I was cast in Doctor Who, I was mainly known as an impressionist, a Saturday night variety person doing musical turns. But I was called in to the production office to meet John Nathan-Turner and his (as I realised afterwards) partner, Gary, who was the floor manager. John, as everyone in the business knew, was so camp he could make Christopher Biggins look like Bruce Willis.

There he was, sitting in his beautiful, colourful Hawaiian shirt, with resplendent, bejewelled hands, and the first words he spoke to me were: "I just wanted to say, we saw you on Tarby & Friends at the weekend, doing that incredible spot. We thought anyone who can transform herself into Judy Garland has got to be able to do a werewolf."

That was the nub of it. They wanted a girl who could go from punk lost soul, via moonlight, into a werewolf, as a sort of a metaphor for the star turn. I had to do a bit of crawling along the floor and howling for the director, to convince him I had the acting chops for it, but basically it was a done deal.

After that, I became a good friend of John and Gary, and their little circle down in Brighton. What I loved about *The Greatest Show in the Galaxy* was that we had a gloriously eclectic band of star players; the fantastic Peggy Mount (she'd played the fairy godmother on my first ever panto), T P McKenna (the last of the hellraisers), Ian Reddington (later famously in EastEnders) and Gian Sammarco (from the TV version of Adrian Mole). Sophie Aldred and I just hit it off straight away. Our birthdays are just a few weeks apart, so we are almost exactly the same age.

"Anyone who can transform herself into Judy Garland has got to be able to do a werewolf."

It's quite well-known that we had to film that story in the car park at Elstree Studios. It was the original guerilla TV, a pop-up circus tent in the back and a "the show must go on" attitude. It was in the 25th anniversary year and we filmed it at the start of an early summer, so it has stayed with me as a golden memory. We did kind of realise, even as we did it, it was a very special time.

A couple of years ago I picked up my sketch book and started drawing. I'd been working with Phill Jupitus on tour in Spamalot, and he had a look at my stuff and suggested I start work on a graphic novel. Now I'm meeting all these people in the comic book industry and there is a cross-over of interest. I met another artist, a girl who has done a lot of Doctor Who illustrations for magazines, and when she found out I'd played Mags she went nuts. So who knows, maybe there's a market for a spin-off about when Ace and Mags teamed up and went off to have adventures on another planet?

Michael Grade

Baron Grade of Yarmouth,
former controller of BBC1
*"Axed" Doctor Who from BBC TV
schedules in 1985*

I cancelled it! I killed the bastard! I just didn't
realise it was immortal.

I was presented with the Horse's Ass award, which I still
keep: a little plastic gilded horse's arse which was sent to me
from the Doctor Who Appreciation Society of America. They also
issued a handkerchief with my face on it in the hope that fans
would blow their noses on me.

There are these people who, wonderfully, live and breathe it and
it's a cult. But you can't build a mass TV audience with a cult.

I've never cared for science fiction, except for maybe Quatermass
and Close Encounters. I never got Star Wars at all. I admired it but
it did not engage me. Similarly, Doctor Who was not for me, not
my taste at all. (Mind you, if I'd exer-

> **"I killed the bastard!
> I just didn't realise it
> was immortal."**

cised my taste as a channel controller
over the years a lot of shows would
never have happened.)

I cancelled it. It was absolutely the
right decision at the time. My argument
with the producer was that the same audience watching Doctor
Who was watching Star Wars and E.T. The show was ghastly. It
was pathetic. It just got more and more violent; they resorted to
the most horrific hangings. It was just horrible to watch. It lost
its way.

It was waiting for Russell T Davies.

Russell brought such imagination to it; now the production
values are high, the scripts are witty, it's full of invention. And
digital effects today enable you to do so much more. The
only connection it has with its previous life is the title and the
premise, but it's light years ahead.

I've got a young son, he's now 12 and we watched it from the beginning, I thought he might enjoy it and I was interested to see what was done with it. He was captivated and I could see this was a really special, brilliant piece of work by Russell and the team involved. I thought it was sensational.

So yes, I'm pleased that the show's back and in such good health, it was a brave decision to bring it back. But Russell is unquestionably a massive, massive, talent — if he'd said he was going to do it, and with such enthusiasm, even I would have commissioned it.

Richard Briers

Actor
Played the brother of Tom Baker's character in Monarch of the Glen

I'm going to try to remember for you this tremendous bit of acting I did with Mr Sylvester McCoy. It was such a long time ago but I did see a recording of it only about 10 years ago and I thought it was rather splendid.

> **"They worked so hard, and it was such a terribly frightening series at times."**

Now, the BBC were kind of gunning for Doctor Who around that time. They wouldn't leave it alone. But Sylvester is a very good actor, and we did very well. We had a lot of laughs backstage — such a nice man, he was. He was a prankster. He was always over the top with himself, and fun. He's played with the Royal Shakespeare Company — in King Lear, as the fool, and he played the spoons, which was marvellous against Ian McKellen.

Now the one I was in, about a future tower block, wasn't too far off where we are today. Of course, I absolutely had to play the old chap who came in — the Chief Caretaker — as Hitler. The producer, John Nathan-Turner, I know was very young, and he had become a bigger and bigger fish as far as producers were concerned.

I was with Clive Merrison, a very good actor who played many parts on the radio, including Richard III and Sherlock Holmes.

He's very well known. He was my sidekick, as the caretaker. We were reading the paper and eating sandwiches when we saw the producer was talking very softly with the director. He seemed to be looking at me with some rather nasty expressions.

I couldn't believe it. What had happened was that he thought I was over the top. Well, I was playing Hitler! You couldn't get much more over the top. I began to feel glad that this was a fancy, outrageous part. Clive was marvellous, and he cheered me up by saying, "Of course you're perfectly right to do it over the top". Because the man I was playing was insane.

It's such an incredible show, and was so popular in its day. My wife, Ann, even had a part in it with William Hartnell. She actually met a Dalek, and came off best (just about). I think, had it been better financed, maybe the ambition would have been met. There's a fine line between making a Saturday night entertainment show and a hard-hitting drama. They worked so hard, and it was such a terribly frightening series at times, but at least it encouraged people to see a little bit beyond their horizons.

What I think is rather marvellous is that the younger ones who were watching then are looking so beautifully after the show now.

Gary Russell

Writer, director, former script editor on Doctor Who
Appeared in TV Times in 1978 pictured next to a pile of Doctor Who books

"I'm not sure exactly when I became a fan of Doctor Who but..." is a commonly used term — but not for me. Because I know the exact moment I went from, "Oh I like this programme, Ma" to, "I am never missing a single beat of this show ever again, Ma, and if anyone tries to stop me, I will kill them. Slowly. With sharp things and poisons. Or I will cry. A lot."

"I'm seven, okay, this is bloody brilliant!"

It was the very last shot of episode five of the 1970 story, *Inferno*. For those of you unaware of this classic, basically the world is going to pot 'cos this mad scientist with an indeterminate

European accent and a bad beard is drilling into the Earth's core to release a new gas. (Hello, this was a Britain obsessed with North Sea Gas.) Instead he releases green lava that turns people into monsters (quelle surprise) and the Doctor travels to a parallel Earth where the drilling is far more advanced, where there are more monsters and the scientist's beard is gone. Instead now he wears a white coat, tiny glasses and has an extra letter in his surname.

By the end of this particular episode, an enthralled Gary Russell is utterly engrossed in this whole parallel world thing: Liz Shaw is a brunette not a blonde, the Brigadier has an eye patch and a scar (I'm seven, okay, this is bloody brilliant!) and UNIT are called something else and shoot at the Doctor. The climax has the Doctor and his friends trapped in an office with a window in the door that resembles his dad's shed window and — SMASHH (extra H for parallel world eeek-ness) — a hairy green arm smashes through it, groping out for people. Go theme tune.

Go Gary to his dad's shed and take a long hard stare at that identical window, slightly worried that an equally identical green hairy arm might come through it, but truthfully more hoping that when he goes back outside, he might be in a parallel world where his parents make Doctor Who appear on telly every day rather than once a week, where he'll have no evil older brothers of any kind, and where Nicola Skegg at school will suddenly love Doctor Who as much as he does…

Toby Young
Journalist and author
As a kid, believed his cousin's dad's BBC prop Dalek was real

I remember watching Doctor Who as a child with varying degrees of terror.

"I screamed the house down."

For me, the most horrifying of all the creatures the Doctor had to do battle with were the Silurians. I used to lie awake in bed at night, looking out for their glowing red eyes in the dark. The disturbing thing is that I often saw them — or thought I did.

The first time this happened, I screamed the house down, at which point my mother came rushing in and I forced her to turn on the light to prove that my room was Silurian-free. She then threatened to stop me watching Doctor Who — "You're too young!" — but I managed to convince her it was just a one-off nightmare, rather than a fully-fledged hallucination.

After that, whenever I saw a Silurian in my room — roughly once a night — I had to keep schtum. Better to face the slimy, reptilian creatures alone in the dark than risk not being allowed to watch my favourite TV programme.

Bill Oddie

Author, actor, comedian, artist, naturalist and musician
Played Red Jasper in the audio adventure,
Doctor Who and the Pirates

There are plusses and minuses about being an iconic TV character. I should know. For more than a decade I was a "Goodie". And I still am, even though I haven't ridden a three-seater bike or fought any giant kittens for nearly 30 years. Once a Goodie always a Goodie. And even more so, once a Doctor Who always a Doctor Who.

> **"Troughton came on like a cross between Dracula and the late Hughie Greene."**

Of course the Goodies ceased to exist in 1981, while Doctor Who is still going strong (after a few years in hibernation). However, the two shows are not unconnected — both, for example, continue to enjoy a massive fan base in Australia and New Zealand. The reason for this is not simply that those Down Under have such excellent taste, but that in relatively recent history there was a sort of "British hour" on ABC TV that showed first The Goodies and then Doctor Who, or vice versa, back to back. The result is that millions of 20- and 30-something Antipodeans consider The Goodies and Doctor Who to be equally seminal parts of their childhood or teenage years.

And not one but two Doctor Whos appeared as guest weirdos on The Goodies. This is true.

In 1972, Patrick Troughton played the unforgivably evil and yet desperate-to-be-loved arch villain Dr Wolfgang Adoiphous Rat-Phink Von Petal. The only soupçon of typecasting was that he was also a Doctor. Troughton came on like a cross between Dracula and the late Hughie Greene, thus proving what a fine actor he was.

In addition, abstruse nerdish history records that — also in the early 1970s — Peter Davison made a small appearance in a Goodies episode, but he was surely so young then that he must have needed a chaperone. Did he play a comedy toddler? Maybe he ended up on the cutting room floor. I would like to think that we inspired him to vow, "You may discard me now, but you just wait. One day I will be Doctor Who!" No doubt we laughed. But maybe he could see into the future. Born to play the part!

I would therefore like to take this opportunity to here record, speaking as a Goodie, my debt and thanks to Doctor Who. For letting us borrow a couple of actors, provoking us to send up the Daleks by sticking a sink plunger on a talking dustbin, and for giving us hours and hours of pleasure. We are proud of our, albeit tenuous, associations.

Oh yes, I might just add that, when casting comes up for the next Doctor Who series, all three Goodies, despite their advancing years, are still capable of remembering lines, looking wry or fearful as the scene demands, and being helped and abetted by attractive female assistants. Here's an idea. How about three Doctor Whos, at the same time? Sort of a split personality, but three ways, not just two?

BBC bosses, are you reading this? Come on, before it's too late.

Tara Newley

Actress, writer, singer
Was not named after the planet containing a segment of The Key to Time

They just don't allow people on the set of Doctor Who. Least of all when they're filming an episode as top secret as *The Next Doctor*.

It's almost embarrassing in a way because I know how lucky we were. They really don't let people down there. The show's become so huge and so popular, and there are a million and one people who would have loved to be in our place. So we were all very aware that we were getting a very special experience. We were in Cardiff for just a couple of hours, but it was a dream of a lifetime, and Mum was only too happy to open the doors.

Mum? Okay, she's perhaps better known outside our house as Joan Collins.

Now I hate to burst your bubble but I don't recall my mother being a huge sci-fi fan. My brother Sacha and I used to watch it as kids (probably with the nanny). But certainly, when we went to the Doctor Who set, she got into the fun of it and tried on some of the prosthetics. We went into some of the special effects rooms — as a grandmother she was more carried away by the enthusiasm of her grandchildren, who are obviously enormous Doctor Who fans, to the nth degree.

> **"We were all very aware that we were getting a very special experience."**

My daughter Miel had eyes painted on her hands like the soothsayers in *The Fires of Pompeii*. And, of course, what Weston wanted was his hair like the Doctor. (He still runs around with a sonic screwdriver and likes to comb his hair back saying he looks like Doctor Who.) We watched them film a scene in a two-tier set, saving urchins in Victorian London. I loved sitting on the catering bus, having my lunch with all these Cybermen with half their kit off.

David Tennant was so sweet — I've got a huge crush — he came over and talked to the kids. My son chatted to "the Doctor" for 10 minutes but I still don't think he understood the correlation between character and performer.

I don't think anything can prepare you for the fact that the show is so monumentally awesome these days. I have to keep saying, "We were so lucky to go there that one time — it ain't going to happen again!"

Unless… Mum?

Richard Herring

Comedian, podcaster and writer
*Played a victim of the Cybermen in the BBC webcast,
Real Time*

Growing up in the 1970s meant that Doctor Who played an enormous part in my childhood. I certainly recall Jon Pertwee as the Doctor — his assistant Jo was my first crush, when I was much too young to make any sense of those feelings and why I enjoyed seeing her climbing in through that window in *The Sea Devils*. It was as exciting and terrifying as any of the monsters.

But it was Tom Baker's Doctor and Elisabeth Sladen's Sarah Jane who became my Doctor and assistant. Sarah Jane, though less overtly sexy than Jo (or maybe because of that), quickly replaced her in my affections. And it was the right decision. Elisabeth Sladen never posed naked hugging a Dalek like that slattern Katy Manning.

> **"I am reminded of the series whenever I open a box of Weetabix."**

More weirdly, perhaps, I am reminded of the series whenever I open a box of Weetabix and am greeted by the distinctive combined smell of wheat biscuit and cardboard.

In 1975, this cereal had an amazing Doctor Who promotion. The back of each packet was a diorama of a fantastical alien world or the inside of the TARDIS, while inside were four cardboard figures from the series to pop out, stand up and play with. I was seven years old and collecting these figures was an obsession for me.

In the 21st century with hi-tech toys and computer games it's hard to believe that a child could have got so much pleasure from some frankly quite badly drawn and ridiculous characters on bits of cardboard, but I really did. I suspect that, if you were nerdy enough, yet also grown up enough to store pristine copies at the time, you could be sitting on a fortune. But only if you managed to collect them all. I'm pretty sure that the Ogron and the White Robot were never in my possession. But maybe it is only right that I played with these bits of card until they fell apart, or ripped them up in a passionate moment of play.

Thinking about them again takes me back to the kitchen of my home in Loughborough in 1975. I was due to leave the next year to live out the rest of my childhood in Somerset and don't have many memories connected to that house. But these figures have transported me through time to half-remembered places. Which I suppose is rather apt.

Katy Manning

Actress, played the Doctor's companion Jo Grant
Wore a fake beard for the studio read-through of Colony in Space

Those of us who go back 40 years or so know that Dick Emery was a very popular comedian then and had the most amazing show. He was the real "hot dude" at the time and used to dress up as a woman who said, "Ooh you are awful, but I like you!" He was a good friend of Jon Pertwee's — as everybody seemed to be.

Jon had a motorbike and we used to love going to rehearsals on it. When it corresponded with the days that Dick Emery was in the studios, Jon would pick me up outside the house on his motorbike, and we'd have a burn-up with Dick Emery to see who could get to Television Centre first! It was always great fun doing that and a lovely way to arrive. I was the Ton-Up Girl back then. We nearly always won.

> **"Jon Pertwee was my hero in real life too."**

As everyone knows, Jon was absolutely mad about all kinds of machinery. I'll never forget *Day of the Daleks* when we disappeared on the three-wheeler and bumped our way around the countryside.

Talk about memories!

Mind you, on my very first day at Television Centre, Prince Charles opened the door for me, smiled and said, "Hello!"

In the rehearsal room, Jon and I had a toy drawer which consisted of coloured pencils, bits of paper, funny little toys, chocolate cream eggs… loads of kids' stuff, really. I said to him one day,

"Supposing we didn't have any arms and we painted with our feet?" So — and this was probably a terribly politically incorrect thing to do — we did some painting. We took our shoes and socks off in the lunch hour and we just sat there with bits of paper on the floor doing foot painting!

And the next day, the cleaners had thrown all Jon's away but mine were still there!

Of course, when you're in the studios, they're doing the much more complex special effects, so things took longer. We'd spend wonderful hours sat in that cupboard of a TARDIS! Jon was so full of stories, and we used to play a lot of word games together. Those are the sort of memories that I really do treasure — the fact that Jon was always there, you know, at the edge of a cliff in case I ran over. He'd be there to stop me. He was my hero in real life too!

John Challis

Actor
Played mercenary henchman Scorby in The Seeds of Doom *(and Boycie in Only Fools and Horses)*

I first watched Doctor Who when William Hartnell was the Doctor, in the early 1960s. He was totally convincing as the Time Lord and I could never envisage anyone else doing it better. I was only 21 or so and I found it a bit scary sometimes, but I'd watch with a girlfriend so I had an excuse to put a comforting arm around her!

I worked a lot in the theatre in those days and I couldn't help noticing that the scenery was a bit dodgy most of the time. They used a lot of polystyrene, and rocks would sometimes float about. All the different Doctors have had their moments and wildly different qualities, but Tom Baker has to be my favourite. (He'd kill me if I said otherwise!) I just loved his eccentricity. Luckily I have the DVD of *The Seeds of Doom*, but only because the BBC kindly sent me a copy. So, of course, that is my favourite story, not only because I am part of such a great adventure but because I had the time of my life filming it.

I have two original copies of the Target book Doctor Who and The Seeds of Doom with fantastic artwork by Chris Achilleos. One was sent to me by a fan and the other I found at a memorabilia fair. People send me photos of me as Scorby but goodness knows where they come from, because the BBC haven't got any. I would love a photo of me and Tom together but that doesn't seem likely. I've nothing left to remind me of the programme because everything's been signed and sent out to charities over the years, including my drip-dry statue of Tom Baker!

> **"Tom Baker is one of the great characters in our business."**

Tom is one of the great characters in our business and I got on very well with him. We shared a weird sense of humour. He used to love my impression of James Stewart and one day, many years later, I met him in Soho and we stopped to chat on a street corner. He asked me to do Jimmy one more time and laughed like a drain. Just then, two workmen passed us and did a double take: "Cor, blimey! That's not something you see every day. Boycie doing Jimmy Stewart talking to Doctor Who!"

Kerry Wilkinson

Author of Locked In, UK #1 Amazon Kindle bestseller
Got married in a copycat David Tennant suit, complete with white trainers

I was always a reader as a child but we never had much money. I would pick up the thin Target books from various charity shops and tear through them in a day. At the time, I didn't even realise Doctor Who was a television programme. One evening, I saw a Dalek on the screen and suddenly it all became clear. My parents had managed to keep it from me because of all the media hysteria that used to float around about how scary it was.

> **"I've never been so scared and thrilled."**

I vaguely remember parts of *Remembrance of the Daleks* but my first full memory of Doctor Who is *The Greatest Show in the Galaxy*, which pretty much proved my parents' point. I still remember sitting on the floor in the living room watching Jessica Martin as Mags transform into a werewolf. I'm not sure I've ever been so scared and thrilled at the same time.

I've never watched it back since, though. I suspect it hasn't aged well.

I've also never forgotten the vampire girls with the long nails from *The Curse of Fenric*, which just goes to show how these things live with you. The problem, for a nine-year-old desperate for more, was that the programme then disappeared from our screens for years. I did, however, save my money and buy every New Adventures book as they came out throughout my teenage years which, as you might imagine, was an absolute winner with the girls…

Thank God it came back and everyone watches now — even my wife. I still have those New Adventures too, all first editions and many now worth a small fortune because of the small print runs. Not that I'd sell, of course!

Rufus Hound

Comedian and presenter
Had a Dalek tattooed onto his left bicep in 2007

The life of a jobbing comedian is not as glamorous as the legends would have you believe. Sure, earning a living for a daily 20 minutes' work is lovely, but that 20 minutes usually comes at a cost of several hours driving, possibly a stay overnight, and the long drive back the next day.

So it was that I found myself in the Birmingham Holiday Inn, conveniently situated next to the one-way system's finest 24-hour kebab shop and car stereo test facility. The people of Birmingham are great, but Birmingham itself can be a bit bleak. In preparation, I'd recorded the two episodes of Doctor Who I'd missed by being on the road. They were *Silence in the Library* and *Forest of the Dead*.

I should point out, I am not one of those Doctor Who fans. I am not hugely familiar with the Whoniverse pre-Eccleston. I cannot draw the Seal of Rassilon from memory, I cannot tell you which part

Martin Clunes played (though you'd think I would from the number of "embarrassing clips" shows it's been on) and I could walk past Patrick Troughton in the street without so much as pausing. A task made all the trickier by his passing away some 22 years ago.

"On that day, in that place, I cried for every lost child of Gallifrey."

But in that boxy, street-noisy hotel room the double bill of *Silence/Forest* changed everything. My day, my outlook, my emotional integrity. I don't want to run through the plot, the excellent performances or the moral of the story. You may have seen them (if you're reading this, I reckon there's probably a good chance you can quote large sections of it) or you may not have done, but what is true is that these episodes encapsulate everything that is most wonderful about this series.

I hated Steven Moffat and I loved him. So brilliantly clever, so horribly cruel, so incredibly redeemed. That the Doctor should be forced to recognise his soul mate, then be responsible for her ascent to digital heaven is to fully exploit the unique opportunities that writing for Doctor Who affords you. It is no lie that the Doctor's last minute dash to immortalise River Song was accompanied in that Birmingham hotel room by a sobbing moustachioed man-child shouting "Run! F***ing run!" at a glowing laptop screen, unafraid and unashamed of who might hear.

There in a soulless Holiday Inn I sat, with tears streaming down my face, weeping inconsolably. On that day, in that place, I cried for every lost child of Gallifrey.

As the story ended, I felt rattled, euphoric and spent. There are a few things that a man alone in a hotel room can do to induce these feelings, but none of them should be done while crying. And none of them will ever make you feel that every switch in your head and heart has been jammed on and cranked up. None of them will make you want to write a letter to Moffat that simply reads, "You bastard. You beautiful bastard."

And none of them will make you want to call your own wife just to tell her that you love her and miss her and if she ever kills herself to save you, you'll upload her to heaven.

Chris Limb

Writer, designer

Son of Roger Limb of the BBC Radiophonic Workshop

I walked through the doors, pushed through a heavy black velvet curtain and suddenly found myself standing on the surface of an alien world. I was on Traken. Or rather I was in a studio at the BBC on the set of *The Keeper of Traken*.

A lot had changed for the Doctor at that time. The series was undergoing a metamorphosis, similar to that experienced at the end of the Pertwee era. The old Doctor was again having to cope with a style of programme that would become his successor's stock in trade. The opening sequence had changed and, even more shockingly, Delia Derbyshire's definitive arrangement of the theme tune had been replaced by a new, more modern version, realised by the Radiophonic Workshop.

This last modification was the reason I'd ended up here. Producer John Nathan-Turner had decided to involve the Workshop to a greater extent than just "special sounds", with the result that my dad had been asked to compose some of the incidental music. The first serial he worked on was *The Keeper of Traken* so, when it started filming, he was able to bring me along to the set.

For some reason, the Traken palace shared studio space with the interior of the Master's TARDIS. There it was, over in one corner, roundels sprayed a distinctive black just so you were sure you were looking at an evil version. Rather than a central console it had a flight deck below two eye-shaped viewscreens. And…

"The series was undergoing a metamorphosis."

There was the Master himself, in 13th regeneration rotting corpse mode, chatting to one of the studio staff. There too was Adric, smiling sheepishly in a leather jacket. Over the other side of the studio was the Doctor, looking scary, bad tempered and tall, his burgundy costume hanging off him. And right next to me was my younger brother, Jeremy.

What, I wondered, did he make of all this?

Jeremy Limb

Comedian, actor, musician

Son of Roger Limb of the BBC Radiophonic Workshop

For most people Tom Baker *was* Doctor Who. He was the Platonic ideal of which all previous and subsequent Doctors were merely forms.

Personally, I had never known another Doctor. Faint recollections of tiny moments from Pertwee's last season were degraded, memories of memories, like an umpteenth generation VHS copy. So when our dad took us to the set of *The Keeper of Traken*, I saw *my* Doctor. The hero of my favourite ever TV programme. There he was, standing just a few feet away.

> **"Surely, if I could say hello to anyone, it was him?"**

Suddenly, he turned and started walking straight towards me. What else could I do? I ran and hid.

I've always had an overdeveloped sense of embarrassment about meeting famous people. When they acknowledge your presence it's as if something has gone wrong in the natural order of the universe; once I screamed and hid on the floor of the family car when Jimmy Savile waved at us (although I now know this was the correct, instinctive, response). But the Doctor! Surely, if I could say hello to anyone, it was him?

No, I ran and hid. He looked scary, aloof, forbidding. In retrospect we now know he was going through a difficult time – with his (then) wife Lalla, with the production team, with his feelings as he approached the end, however much it had been prepared for. Maybe if I had said hello he would've taken the time to squat down, grin and ask my name in his comforting, bread-like voice, like he had done with so many other nine-year-old boys... but instead, my chief memory of that eventful day is of running and hiding from perhaps the most quintessential Doctor of them all.

Still, considering what Doctor Who meant to me, and still means to me, maybe that's actually quite appropriate.

Jenny Colgan

Author
Ashamedly hid her TARDIS key ring from David Morrissey at a literary event

WHSmiths were running a competition: "Meet Doctor Who!" All you had to do was enter some totally easy questions and complete the tiebreaker, "I love Doctor Who books because…"

I won't repeat my slightly embarrassing answer here. But winning that competition (the first and last time I have ever won anything) was by some measure the greatest thing that had ever happened to me, beating my first communion into a cocked hat. I was 11 years old.

There then followed months of waiting while the publishers, Smiths and the BBC got their act together, and I moved to secondary school. You can, I imagine, guess how popular being the as yet unrewarded winner of a Doctor Who competition made me among the girls with real bras and make up.

At last, it came — my father marched in one night, beaming with pride and boldly holding aloft the local paper's advertising board which he'd begged off the newsagent — PRESTWICK GIRL TO MEET DOCTOR WHO! And my mother and I were off, swept aboard the London sleeper to a world of adventures!

I still can't believe what my parents made me wear. I was, let's face it, auditioning to be the Doctor's youngest companion ever but there I am in the pics with a hideous boy's haircut and a free — the shame! — adult male's t-shirt advertising guitar strings from my father's music shop. Along with a large pair of khaki shorts (also boy's), brown sandals and bare hairy legs, I never stood a chance.

> **"Winning that competition was the greatest thing that ever happened to me."**

Down into the bowels of Television Centre we went, and into a vast, black space, filled with people anxiously wrapping foam mattresses with silver foil to make space mattresses. There, in the far corner, standing outside the iconic

box as if he'd just popped straight down, was a tall man wearing a stick of celery on his lapel.

Peter Davison wasn't my Doctor, not exactly. My Doctor wore a very long scarf, had an occasionally exasperated bark, and a re-assuring way with a jelly baby. But this would do. I instantly did what was appropriate under the circumstances, and burst into tears.

Tegan and Nyssa (who had left the show but popped in for lunch) were, as you'd expect, incredibly sweet and kind to me after that. Turlough, of whom I was, frankly, terrified, turned out to be a delight. And even the Doctor politely posed for pics (my tear-stained face glinted off the flash) but declined to show me inside the TARDIS ("You'd be very disappointed"). I think he thought I was an eight-year-old boy, not a nearly 12-year-old girl. It didn't matter though. My lifelong devotion was assured.

Richard Freeman

Cryptozoologist
During a spell in hospital, took a portable TV to watch
Genesis of the Daleks *with the nurses*

Doctor Who is the greatest show in the history of TV. Moreover, it made me who I am. I owe Doctor Who my career.

I grew up in the 1970s with Jon Pertwee as the Doctor and the horrors lurking right here on Earth, on our very doorstep; super-evolved marine reptiles; giant maggots; animated killer dolls; huge inter-dimentional spiders. You don't get that in banal dross like Buffy the Vampire Slayer or Star Trek: The Next Generation.

"Some of the creatures I have hunted are not unlike the Doctor's foes."

When I left school, after a few years' zookeeping, a stint as a grave-digger and three years at Leeds University, I became a cryptozoologist (a zoologist that specialises in searching for animals whose existence has not been proven). Currently, I'm also the zoological director of The Centre For Fortean Zoology, the only full-time scientific organisation in the world that actively seeks to investigate unknown animals (or, as modern man labels them, monsters). So, if you want to be melodramatic about it, I am, in essence, a monster hunter! My many expeditions have taken me all over the world — through jungles and swamps, across deserts and up mountains, on the track of weird creatures.

Some of the beasties I have hunted for are not unlike the Doctor's foes over the years. The Mongolian Deathworm is a sausage-shaped creature said to lurk under the sands of the Gobi. We came to the conclusion it was an unknown species of worm lizard. Nomads say it spits a corrosive yellow saliva. So, er, the yellow death, then, rather than *The Green Death*!

The Naga of Indo-China and the Ninki-Nanka of West Africa are crested, serpentine, latter-day dragons. Sightings send whole communities into panic and have been known to empty villages in fear. Shades of the Mara, or maybe the Drashigs?

And, sounding not unlike the Ogrons, the Almasty of the Caucasus Mountains may be a relic hominid, a possible surviving strain of Homo erectus. In 2008, I believe I got to within 12 feet of one of these proto-men on an abandoned farm at 2.30 in the morning! At the time of writing, dung and bones we brought back from Russia are being studied.

No one ever got rich being a cryptozoologist but it's a life of adventure. All this I owe to the man in the Victorian opera cape and frilly shirt.

Simon Guerrier
Writer of books, audio plays and comics
Was the last person filmed in Sarah Jane Smith's attic

The Mara started the nightmares. I was five years old, had been watching Doctor Who for about a year, and I remember vividly.

It didn't help that the bit where the Doctor's friend Tegan gets taken over by the evil snake creature is filmed as if it's a nightmare. There's a pale sort of clown person dancing in the darkness, deep inside Tegan's eye.

As much as it scared me, I couldn't look away. Admit to the nightmares and Mum and Dad would probably not let me watch Doctor Who again. And then I'd never know how the Mara was defeated. So I watched in rapt terror as the Doctor unravelled the weird, nightmarish logic. The Mara hates its own reflection, so he traps it in a circle of mirrors. Now it can't look away…

But the Mara wasn't gone. A year later, it had Tegan all evil again and more nightmares for me. Even when it was defeated, in the next story Tegan isn't sure she'll ever be free of its curse. The Doctor can't promise her it will be okay.

"As much as it scared me, I couldn't look away."

That's in a story called *Mawdryn Undead*, in which a wheezy, bruised creature claims to be the next incarnation of the Doctor. That one got really into my head, partly because I was horrified by the implication of the Doctor having died on his own in a spaceship crash, and his regeneration going wrong. But also actor David Collings gives such a haunting performance.

Doctor Who doesn't give me nightmares any more. But two years ago, I was invited to visit a studio during the recording of an audio play.

And I had to make an excuse. David Collings was in the cast. I didn't quite dare face him.

Emma Freud
Broadcaster and producer
Script-edited her partner Richard Curtis' episode of Doctor Who

Its odd isn't it? Who told the nation's children that, when they were scared by Doctor Who, they should all, collectively, hide behind the sofa? Not the chair, not the curtains, not the door… The sofa. You did it. I did it. How did we know?

A few summers ago, Richard, our four children and I went on holiday to Italy for a month. We rented an old school house on the edge of a village and did that thing the English do on holiday…

Absolutely nothing at all.

Until, that is, the second week, when Richard set up the spare bedroom — we never have guests — as the room of Van Gogh's painting, Bedroom in Arles.

"By day, we took it in turns to write scenes."

We then spent the next fortnight working on the script for *Vincent and the Doctor*. Richard had sketched out the plot but, as a family, we turned it into an episode. By night we watched old Who classics, and by day we took it in turns to write scenes. It was more fun than Monopoly, though possibly just slightly less than Pictionary…

But for all of us it was a privilege to be allowed to write words to be uttered by the men and women of our dreams and nightmares.

Nick Bateman

Writer, broadcaster, "Nasty" Nick from Big Brother
Was terrified of the maggots in The Green Death

Courtesy of the BBC, I now have copies of my two favourite Doctor Who photos. One is of the Cybermen walking down the steps of St. Paul's and the other one is of the Daleks going over Westminster Bridge.

I'd been doing some charity pictures with the Radio Times and I said to the folks there, "Look, there are two photos I'd really like to get hold of." A friend of mine's father worked on the series (or, at least, had something to do with it) and she has the same two pictures on the fridge in her kitchen.

"It's kind of weird to meet a Doctor in the flesh."

The problem with the Dalek one is that, in the corner of the picture, if you look carefully, you can see the shadow of the photographer.

I believe, initially, that Terry Nation created the Daleks as an allegory for the Nazis. Therefore the thing that always sticks in my memory is the absurdity of Tom Baker offering them jelly babies. Presumably, the thinking was that the

Dalek wouldn't quite know what a jelly baby is, so you would blow its circuits.

Speaking of which, if you'd travelled back in time to see me 10 years ago and said, "You'll be having a dinner party with Doctor Who," I'd have replied, "No!" But when I was asked to be on TV's Come Dine With Me, one of the other celebrity guests was none other than Colin Baker.

It's kind of weird to meet a Doctor in the flesh because you want to ask him lots of questions. Yet, at the same time, I'm very mindful of how dull it is to have to answer them; when people meet me, they always ask about Big Brother.

Hmm… meeting somebody who you've watched on telly in the past — and suddenly, there they are, having dinner with you in the future… now that's actually quite "science fiction".

Ed Petrie

Actor, comedian, presenter
Threw hot cross buns at Karen Gillan on CBBC with a talking cactus

One of my earliest memories is of watching Doctor Who while eating fish and chips with my Mum. It was lunchtime and she'd recorded it on our Betamax video recorder (wise technology purchase there, Mum and Dad). Tom Baker was nearing the end of his stint and, in a few episodes' time, I was going to witness his traumatic death from falling off an electricity pylon. Yes, geeks, I know it wasn't an electricity pylon but, in my underdeveloped child's brain, I somehow thought it was. From that point on I held the pylons running alongside the dual carriageway between Rustington and Goring personally responsible for the death of the lovely, curly-haired Doctor.

"I thought Margaret Thatcher declared war on Tegan."

Anyway, the Doctor's new companion was introduced to me this episode. And because — as we have already established — I was an idiot, I somehow got her name confused with the country Argentina. In my defence, I was just over two and a half years old.

Unlike Tom Baker, Tegan gave the pylon a wide berth and carried on time-travelling with the more health-and-safety-conscious Peter Davison. And on one occasion she pranced around in a bikini that made me feel funny. (Or was that Peri? Frankly, I've got better things to do with my time than trawl through every episode with Tegan and Peri in hoping to find the moment I first realised I quite liked bikini clad women, but maybe I'll get round to it when I'm retired.)

When I was about four years old, Margaret Thatcher declared war on Argentina. I caught something on the news about this, probably after an episode of Grange Hill I wasn't supposed to be watching, and thought she was declaring war on Tegan off Doctor Who. I've never voted Conservative since.

Shaun Dingwall

Actor, played Rose Tyler's father, Pete
Aged six, was wrapped up in the Doctor's scarf by Tom Baker himself

It involves snot.

It may not be the most obvious reply when asked, "What's your favourite Doctor Who moment?" But it is mine.

It's the Cybermen for me. Always has been, probably always will be. It's the old Daleks vs Cybermen cliché but, whenever I whittle it down, it was those metallic, hulking clunk-buckets that, as a kid, guaranteed me nightmares.

So, 25 years later, after taking on the role that is Pete Tyler and driving around town in a 1987 Ford Escort Estate, wearing an ill-fitting polyester suit, I found myself on set again, face to face with a Cyberman.

Actually, that's a lie. It was more like face to chest. Or Cyberboob. This particular Cyberman was nigh on six feet five inches tall. The costume, it transpired, took approximately 45 minutes to climb into. The helmet alone took 15 minutes, with several nuts and bolts to be tightened and locked off. If you got an itchy nose you were buggered, cybernetically speaking.

So, finally, here was the opportunity to meet my childhood demon in the flesh. 25 years ago, I have no doubt that I would have run screaming in search of the nearest chenille three-piece suite

"It was those metallic, hulking clunk-buckets that guaranteed me nightmares."

to dive behind, so I have to confess that I was actually a bit nervous. When you see them in real life they are genuinely intimidating. "I'm an adult," I told myself. "A grown up. Sort of." I would confront my fear.

"Excuse me?" I asked, my throat slightly tightening. "Do you know where the tea urn is?"

No reply. His huge frame remained still, rock solid. His face — with that classic, impassive expression — was unnerving.

Still no reply.

It was a pause of Pinteresque proportions, an epic silent response that screamed power...

Then, ever so slowly, his massive shoulders crept up to his ears, his head rocked slowly back, propelled itself forward like a piston... and a tiny little sneeze discharged from behind the mask.

"Oh heck!" he squealed. "It's a snotfest behind this mask. It's going to be a long night."

Tom Harris
Labour Party MP
Drunkenly told John Simm he would be great as the next Doctor

I have never yet met an actual, real-life Doctor. But it's not for the want of trying.

My first attempt was in 1979. The Target novelisation of *The Horror of Fang Rock* had just been published and Tom Baker was appearing at a Glasgow store to sign copies. Trouble was, I lived nearly 20 miles from Glasgow and, together with my fellow Doctor Who fan and best friend, Brem, I had taken a trip up to the big city a week before and blown both our savings. That was a hard lesson. My next opportunity to meet the lead actor wouldn't present itself for another 28 years.

Along with many other MPs, I was invited to a preview at the Science Museum of 2007's Christmas special, *Voyage of the Damned*. After the question-and-answer session, we were herded to another part of the building where we were served copious Moscow Mules, outnumbered only by the celebs, both Who-related and non-Who-related. My old mate Steven Moffat was there with his wife, Sue Vertue, and he told me he expected Peter Davison to turn up later.

"I chatted with Tony Head, who was quite interested in trams."

I chatted with Tony Head who, as well as having auditioned for the part of the Doctor in the 1996 movie and starring in the Doctor Who episode, *School Reunion*, was quite interested in trams. I was, at the time, minister for said mode. By the time we'd finished talking transport, David Tennant had already left. And Davison didn't turn up either. Yet another opportunity slipped through my fingers, just as the Key to Time evaded the grasp of the Black Guardian at the end of *The Armageddon Factor*.

A few short weeks later, Steven texted me to ask if my wife and I wanted to go over to his house in Kew to watch *Silence in the Library*, written by him and being broadcast as part of the new series' fourth season. Sadly, we weren't able to be in London that weekend, so we passed, but, about a month afterwards, Steven and Sue joined me in the Commons for dinner.

"What a pity you and Carolyn couldn't come over the other week," said Steven. "David and Georgia were there..."

Georgia Moffet, daughter of Peter Davison, and David Tennant. Together! And I'd missed them. Not since Adric died had I been so close to tears. So close, so close...

So here I am, a fan for over 40 years, having still never met my Doctor. But I'll do it one day. Oh, yes... Nothing can stop me now. *Nothing*! Bwah, ha, ha, ha...

Ben Aaronovitch

Author and screenwriter
Could not bring himself to kill off Brigadier Lethbridge-Stewart in the TV story, Battlefield

Doctor Who arrived in my life as a fragmented series of monochrome images — here a terrifying robotic figure, or sinister shape, there a screaming girl running through an endless labyrinth of tunnels. In my memories these fragments suddenly coalesced into the horrific… "figure" is not quite the right word… *form* of a giant maggot.

The story was Malcom Hulke's searing indictment of late stage capitalism, otherwise known as *The Green Death*. My parents couldn't afford a colour TV back then and I think that helped disguise the terrible CSO (colour separation overlay). In my dreams, of course, there were no dodgy special effects. As Stephen King points out in his book, Danse Macabre, in our nightmares we never see the zipper up the monster costume's back.

Then all at once, in my memories at least, it's as if the complete understanding of the show had been downloaded directly into my brain. When the next series started I understood it perfectly. There was this guy who, with his friend, got into a blue box called the TARDIS and went places and did stuff — exciting stuff. It really was that simple.

> **"The Doctor gives himself licence to upturn people's lives."**

In format, Doctor Who most resembles the classic detective: he, or (possibly, by the time you're reading this) she, arrives at a location and proceeds to deal with difficult and interesting situations. The Doctor gives himself licence to upturn people's lives, ferret out their deepest secrets and ignore their social mores — all in the name of bringing order from chaos. Whether that is solving a murder mystery on a Sandminer or preventing the Daleks from conquering the galaxy (again).

Unlike most characters in modern drama, the classic detective rarely undergoes the dreaded "character development" so beloved of executives with no actual feel for story. The detective acts upon the world, not the other way round. Morse starts his career as a lonely, over-educated, opera loving snob and remains like that until he dies. Poirot does not change, nor does Frost, Dalgleish or Charles Paris. The Doctor is the same. Once he has regenerated he retains that personality until he regenerates again. To my mind his lack of character development is a feature, not a bug.

But Doctor Who, the TV series, had two major advantages over even the most beloved of all the classic detectives. One: the fact that he can regenerate means that the series constantly refreshes itself. The Doctor remains, to use another word beloved of executives, relevant. The Doctor never becomes a relic of a bygone age — he is always of the now. He does not so much conform to the zeitgeist as help shape it.

The second advantage Doctor Who has over even the most fanciful detective (I'm looking at you, Sherlock) is the TARDIS. The TARDIS is more than a time machine, it is a delivery mechanism of unparalleled power. It can take your main character and his trusty companions and literally send them anywhere in time and space that your budget will allow.

No other series on television grants its writers this breathtaking scope for action. It is a great and terrifying prospect and one to be seized with both hands.

Eric Wallace

Screenwriter, videogame and comic book author
Met Jon Pertwee at a Doctor Who convention in Austin, Texas in 1985

I discovered Doctor Who shortly after my fourteenth birthday. My inaugural viewing turned out to be a condensed version of *Terror of the Zygons*. I tuned in halfway and was shocked to see octopus people using the Loch Ness Monster to destroy London. It was, without question, the strangest show I had ever seen. Plus, I had no idea who the lead character was or what a police box was. Not that any of this mattered. I instantly fell in love with the programme. Why? I have no idea. But…

I just got it.

Most of my classmates at the time, however, did not. These were the 1980s and they cited elements such as "the effects aren't as good as Star Wars" and "all the characters talk funny" as reasons for their dislike. A tiny part of me sympathised with their concerns, but the rest of me didn't care. I was in love with the stories, which were — without exception — brilliant, fantastic, wonderful, take-you-to-anywhere-or-anytime science fiction tales in which anything could happen.

"Octopus people using the Loch Ness Monster to destroy London."

Back then, Doctor Who was shown on PBS, the Public Broadcasting Service, an American home to such grown-up, comma-endowed titles as I, Claudius and Upstairs, Downstairs. So, to my young mind, if Doctor Who was also on PBS, ergo it must *also* be serious drama. Maybe that was the "it" I instantly got: from an American perspective, classic Doctor Who was Masterpiece Theater with monsters.

It took a few months but I eventually stopped trying to convince my friends that they were missing out on the best science fiction show ever. After that, I just concentrated on enjoying, well, the best science fiction show *ever*. I've been hiding behind the couch ever since. (That's what you guys call a sofa, right?)

Gary Delaney

Comedian
Wanted to invent a Doctor Who monster that could disguise itself as a sofa

I guess the interesting thing about my favourite Doctor Who memory is that it might not be real.

When I was a kid in the 1970s, mom would cut my hair herself to save money: just pop a bowl on, trim the edge with scissors. I like to think I was very much 1976's Justin Bieber (or possibly the fat one from the Double Deckers). Like all socially awkward males of the future I was a Doctor Who fan, but what I saw through my child's eyes was 10 times as amazing as what was actually on the screen. Imagination gave it leverage.

This is probably heresy but I don't revisit classic Who because I know reality can never live up to my memories. My most vivid memory was of monsters that were essentially cloaked figures without any heads. I don't remember what they were called but I was terrified.

I was watching this episode perched on a high stool in the front room as mom cut my hair. I've always been a terrible fidget, much to her annoyance. She'd tried everything to get me to sit still, with no success. Then, that day, she hit on the one thing that worked. She pointed at the screen and said "You know how they lost their heads, don't you? Fidgeting whilst having their hair cut," while ominously making snipping motions with the scissors.

That was it. I didn't want to become a monster. I never again moved during a haircut. I still don't. Not that my mom still cuts my hair. I'm tempted at this point to pick up the phone, call my friend, comic Toby Hadoke, and ask what these monsters were. In fact, I think of asking whenever I see him but I never have, as I suspect the real truth is much more mundane than what I remember and will only disappoint.

> **"My most vivid memory was of cloaked figures without any heads."**

There may well never have been any cloaked headless figures, but there were for me.

Incidentally, I don't think the terrors I remember were the same as the Headless Monks in *A Good Man Goes to War* but I guess it's possible. These more recent creations were far less scary. Partly because, at the time of watching, I was nearly 40, and partly because I recognised the Fat Gay Married Anglican Marine as being Charlie Baker (another comic), who I worked with the week before in Jongleurs Portsmouth.

That sort of stuff never happens when you're five.

Pat Galea
Director and engineer at Icarus Interstellar
Fourth word he learned to spell was "TARDIS"

How did I become a starship engineer? It all began in the early 1970s with a black-and-white television set that turned into a monster.

"Starship engineering is fun."

I suppose at some time our TV must have looked (and worked) like any other TV of the day, but I don't remember it in that state. Over the years it developed a personality and appearance unmatched by any other appliance.

As the set became more unreliable, the risk grew that we would miss an episode of Doctor Who. To prevent this calamity we called on my uncle John, who was a huge fan of the Time Lord, and an electronics genius. He would come to our house with a few tools, and those items he didn't have with him he'd fashion from the materials to hand, such as knitting needles and coat hangers. With his head stuck in the back of the TV, sandwich in one hand, cup of tea in the other, and somehow still managing to poke around the electronics at the same time, he'd shout in his strong Maltese accent, "We've got to get the telly working for Doctor Who!"

We never once missed an episode, though with each additional variable capacitor, potentiometer and exposed wire added to the outside of the set, we increasingly ended up watching the Doctor construct his crazy scientific machines on a TV that was itself growing ever more bizarre.

This early exposure to my uncle's electronics wizardry and the Doctor's hyperspace engineering had a significant impact. I'm now a director of an interstellar research company working on technologies to make starflight a reality. Our craft designs are still smaller on the inside, of course, but even at this primitive stage, starship engineering is fun. It'll take time, but we'll get there.

Ad TARDIS Incrementis!

Nicola Bryant

Actress, played the Doctor's companion Peri Brown
Was given the Trion spaceship prop from her first Doctor Who story, Planet of Fire, *as a souvenir*

It was the last episode of *The Sea Devils* with Jon Pertwee, in 1972. Unlike the previous five episodes that I had watched in the safety and comfort of my own home, the family ventured to the Sussex coast to open up our bungalow for the summer season. Here I was, staring at the sea; the very sea from which the Sea Devils could appear at any moment.

I tried to find the safest place in the room to watch. This involved a great deal of manoeuvring, otherwise my back would have been turned to the beach outside while I faced the television – a position too dangerous to contemplate. So by moving my grandmother to a "more comfortable seat", I secured the safest spot.

> **"Before my eyes its face seemed to transform into a Sea Devil."**

It was a great relief to see the slimy devils destroyed by the good Doctor, never to return — or so I hoped. But in true Doctor Who fashion, my mind could not accept their annihilation entirely. I felt sure they would return to the shore I now inhabited… tonight!

Having delayed bedtime for as long as possible, my sister and I were packed off to our bunk-beds. I couldn't sleep. Our little home was on stilts and underneath my bedroom the rabbits would scamper about. Tonight, their every move signalled the approach of more Sea Devils. They were as frightened as me. The moonlight shone through the thin curtains onto my bed, and in the shadow sat a hideous toy I had been given by my aunt. Before my eyes its face seemed to transform into a Sea Devil. It was one of them! But since it sat at the bottom of my bed next to my ladder, how could I escape?

My sister awoke to my feet thumping onto her bed, as I yelled the word "Run!" But, unlike a Doctor Who story, this exclamation created no response. No one would believe the chameleon-like properties of my stuffed black poodle. This was obviously just another ploy to avoid going to bed.

Instead, I thwarted its evil by reversing the polarity of the neutron flow. Which, roughly translated, meant giving it to the local charity shop the very next day.

Mark Millar

Writer, film producer, creator of Kick Ass
Sat next to an unsuspecting David Tennant at the cinema, watching an Indiana Jones film

I wish I had a great Doctor Who memory from my childhood, but sadly I didn't watch Doctor Who. I watched an amazing amount of dross (from Emu's Broadcasting Company to BJ and The Bear), but somehow never tuned into a single episode of what is surely the best high-concept television series in human history. This poor judgement carried on into my teenage years where I watched Manimal and Automan every single week, but refused my dear old Dad's pleas to watch even one episode of The Singing Detective or Edge of Darkness. Was I an idiot? I'm starting to think so.

> "Nobody in the world ever had a sofa that wasn't pressed up against the wall."

As a child of the Star Wars generation, I ignored Who's brilliant ideas and was always gleefully mocking of the BBC special effects team. Sure, I tuned in for *Logopolis*, but only because it was a cultural event. Thus, my only real memory of the show was a guy in school who phonetically mispronounced it "Doctor Whaugh", ignoring the fact that 'Who" is one of the most commonly used words in the English language. Thinking back, he also called popular British comic 2000 AD "Zooad" so I'm starting to suspect he was vaguely autistic, which makes me feel bad for laughing at the time or even bringing him up now.

So my first real Doctor Who memory, I'm afraid, is *Rose*. Can you believe that? The earliest companion I can remember, at the age of 41, is Billie Piper, and I *know* that makes me one of those despicable Johnny-Come-Latelies you have every right to despise, but my love is no less real, believe me. That Godfather of Geek,

Russell T Davies, just found a mainstream hook I'd never seen before and reeled me in to such an extent that I've since bought all the box-sets and can now easily tell my Sontarans from my Sutekh, thank you very much.

Am I being too honest for a book aimed at Doctor Who zealots? I dunno. But I always hated those documentaries where a string of C-list TV stars tell you how much they love something their agents Googled for them only moments before; where your Kate Thorntons or Nick Hancocks would tell you about hiding behind the sofa as soon as they heard the theme tune, when nobody in the world has *ever* had a sofa that wasn't pressed up against the wall.

So, yeah, my earliest memories are *Love & Monsters* and *Blink* and *Father's Day* and *The Empty Child*, but you'll just have to trust me that I'm now as obsessed with Doctor Whaugh as the rest of you.

Stephen Merchant

Comedian and writer
Wrote the word "geek" on every page of his friend Johnny's copy of Doctor Who Magazine

I was a *big* fan of Doctor Who in the days of Tom Baker — I had the comics, the books, a couple of toy Daleks and so on — but I don't really remember specific episodes. I think I was just dazzled by Tom Baker's performance. Eccentric, wild, very funny. Who knows why I related to a tall, weird-looking bloke with bad dress sense?

I'd sit there, sucking a thumb (usually mine) transfixed. I always thought the Doctor was a great creation, essentially Sherlock Holmes in space, travelling around, solving crimes. Alongside Fozzie Bear and the Fonz he was one of my heroes growing up. Those were the three posters on my bedroom wall. I was so cool.

"I once tried to make my own K-9."

The girl companions weren't that interesting to me back in the 1970s but I loved K-9. I once tried to make my own K-9. I think I'd found the blueprints in a book of Doctor Who monsters or something but instead of doing the sensible thing and getting sheets of wood and hammering them together, I decided I was going to carve the whole thing out of a single block of wood. I went in the shed, got a chisel, chipped out one chunk, almost took my thumb off, got scared and instantly gave up. I don't know why my parents were letting me play with chisels in the shed. I think they were just happy I was out of the house.

I was never really scared during Doctor Who and it never occurred to me that the show looked a bit cheap until I grew up a bit. By my teens I had moved onto other things but nowadays I always watch the Christmas episodes. I like the fact they spend big money on it and they've made the Doctor a bit sexier and cool. If truth be told I'm not as excited about it now as I was when I was a kid. But I'm still afraid of chisels.

Andrew Harrison

Music journalist, former editor of Q, Select and Mixmag
Wept like a weed when Matt Smith appeared with Orbital at Glastonbury in 2010

My earliest memory of Doctor Who is, I think, my earliest memory of anything at all. It's 1972, I'm five years old and I've finally steeled myself to face my fear. There is a programme on telly at teatime on Saturdays that my cousins and friends talk about in hushed tones. Grown-ups don't approve — much too frightening for kids, a bit violent, it'll give them nightmares. I want to watch, and I daren't. I'm still young enough for the wall between the real and the imaginary to be a permeable one. But you can't put these things off forever.

> **"The music made it clear that something terrible had just happened."**

So it's a Saturday night in March 1972, and through the crack in our front room door I'm watching a shambling squadron of turtle-faced man-reptiles lurch out of the sea as a man who looks like Satan himself laughs in triumph. As for the rest of the moment, I've forgotten all of it (were my brothers there in our semi in the suburbs of Liverpool? Did my mum leap to turn the TV off?

No remotes in those days). Events on the screen had eclipsed everything. The music — atonal, sinister, inhuman but fascinating — made it clear that something terrible had just happened. Mankind was definitely, definitely doomed. The Sea Devils, the Master, Jo Grant, extras in soldier outfits dying by the score… and the Doctor. I was hooked, forever.

(Imprinted, in fact. A few years later, in that same front room, I watched Linx the Sontaran scout reveal his face at the exact moment that I took a bite of teatime peanut butter on toast. Ever since I've been unable to separate Sontarans from peanut butter. They even look like they're made of the stuff!)

Memory will always cobble its broken bits into something coherent if completely inaccurate. Somehow, in my head, *The Sea Devils* has been mashed together with another alien spectacle from about the same time: David Bowie performing Space Oddity on Top of the Pops in full "Man Who Fell to Earth" gear. Wispy, gauzy dancers, Vaseline on the lens, an atmosphere of utter alienness that could be the swamps of Spiridon, or the wilds of Peladon, or the plains of Metebelis Three.

In my mind it all became part of the same thing. And it set me on my way: towards music, mystery, and the delicious sense that there is always something amazing nearby, if we could only peek beneath the surface.

Kristin Hersh

Songwriter, founder of US indie band, Throwing Muses
Wanted to be touched by a Weeping Angel

The Doctor was my dad. Or my dad was the Doctor, I'm not sure which. They looked alike and people called Dad "Doctor" for what seemed to me to be flimsy reasons. So I figured those were our home movies with the monsters made out of stuff we found in the back of the garage and the cheap lasers. I knew we were poor and couldn't afford the expensive lasers rich kids' dads shot bubble wrap and mop-head monsters with.

My father had to use science to outwit evil garbage cans 'cos his weapons and spaceships were so crappy. But that made him cooler than the rich dads, cooler than the rich TV stars, cooler than real doctors who only seemed interested in listening to heartbeats. Peering into your life through a keyhole positioned on the outside is a striking thing to do. Science measures everything; it can't help it. It measures your heartbeats — which're pretty goddamn repetitive and therefore boring, no matter what gross love songs tell you — and it measures your wild adventures. The Doctor's adventures are yours through this universal keyhole and you know it, whether you're sitting on your couch or racing around, all tense and terrified. Weirdness is everywhere and it's always about to kick in. It's probably sitting in the back of your garage right now, waiting to strike: *cool*.

> **"Weirdness is everywhere and it's always about to kick in."**

One little shift in your parameters like this, one little shift in your perception (like: right next to the shop on the corner is eternity and eternity is homemade!) means that our adventures only start with our heartbeats. Then they ooze into surrounding tissues and crawl out of our ears onto the couch, eventually body-slamming us within inches of our lives and sanity. And what saves you from facing your mortality? Morality, of course! Every time... that and a cheap old two-bit laser you taped together yesterday afternoon.

Now we know the micro and the macro, the small picture and the big one. We're all visible through the same keyhole, those of us with pounding hearts.

Bob Fischer

BBC Tees radio presenter
Wrote sci-fi convention travelogue, Wiffle Lever to Full!

It's October 1991, and I'm 18 years old, thin as a rake, covered in acne, and utterly terrified. It's my first week at Lancaster University, and I've never felt so out of my depth. My home is the romantically-titled Bowland Annexe, a riot of whitewashed brick walls, freezing tiled floors and a single tiny bathroom shared by 20 students. I'm standing alone in the kitchen eating a fried Smash sandwich, the first stage of a vague plan to commit suicide by cholesterol poisoning.

Suddenly, a light Cumbrian accent chimes in my ear. "Hello," it says. "I'm Gareth."

I lift my head to find a friendly face with a mop of sandy hair looking back at me, smiling. He's a nice lad, softly-spoken and shy, and he invites me back to his tiny room to finish my foul-smelling sandwich. Safe to say my first reaction wasn't quite what he was expecting.

"Bloody hell, there's *The War Games*! And *The Time Warrior*! And *City of Death*!"

Yes, Gareth is a Doctor Who fan. A Doctor Who fan who owns all the videos. A Doctor Who fan who has a TV and a video cassette recorder in his whitewashed student bedroom. He is also bit intimidated by the whole university thing and says, with a hopeful glint in his eye, "We can watch these, if you'd like to…"

"We were introduced by a mutual friend called the Doctor."

So we do. We watch *The War Games* in one sitting, fuelled by Vimto and chocolate digestives. The following night we do *The Deadly Assassin* as horizontal sheets of rain batter against the window. It rains constantly for our first three weeks at university, but we don't care… we're safe together in the Bowland Annexe TARDIS…

17 years later, it's January 2009, and I'm fumbling for my house keys on the drive with frozen fingers. Suddenly, my phone beeps with an unexpected text. It's Gareth.

"He's 26!"

It takes me a second to realise what he's on about. I'm missing the first 10 minutes of Doctor Who Confidential, and Steven Moffat has just revealed the mystery new Eleventh Doctor's age.

Gareth and I are hurtling towards our 40th birthdays now but we're both still good friends. He's still in Lancaster, and I'm back home on Teesside. And when people ask us, "How did you two meet?" the simple, uncomplicated answer is, "At uni". But that's not the whole story. We were introduced by a mutual friend. A friend called the Doctor, who — over two decades ago — brought together two people who might never otherwise have given each other a thought.

He's still my friend as well. And, like Gareth, I think he always will be.

Roland Rat
Superstar
Like the newscaster in The Daemons, *once broadcast on a fictional, but prophetic, BBC Three*

Rodents love Doctor Who, especially me, ratfans, yeahhhhhh!

I have always been a big fan of the show and I love both the movies because of the Daleks! I am a serious Dalek collector and have a large selection permanently on display in my office! I collect old Doctor Who Magazines, the figurines, the 12" dolls. Sevans models were fab, got all them! In fact, you name it, I collect it! Got a lovely battery operated K-9 model from years ago.

My fave Doctor was Patrick Troughton — he was fab, yeahhhh! As a TV legend, I have of course worked with a few Doctors in me time; Colin Baker guested on Roland Rat The Series 'cos my Saturday show went out just before Doctor Who. Worked with Sylvester McCoy — what a lovely man — and Jon Pertwee was an old friend. As we were neighbours, he was going to guest on my show — such a pity that never happened.

"I am a serious Dalek collector."

It's about time I appeared in Doctor Who as a special guest, actually! I can see it now... The Doctor goes back in time and narrowly escapes the Bubonic plague! I'd play the leader of a horde of giant rats infesting Europe that have all had their brains reprogrammed by Davros. I ride around on the back of K-9! Cybermen arrive and attack us all! Hundreds of Daleks join the battle and annihilate everyone apart from me and the Doctor, who then morphs into Megan Fox, the first female Doctor Who! She obviously fancies me and I become the first female Doctor's sidekick and love interest — yeaaahhhhhhhhhhhhhh, perfect!

Bernard Cribbins

Actor

Won a Doctor Who-themed episode of Pointless Celebrities with co-star, Jacqueline King

My first association with Doctor Who was in 1966, in one of the feature films with Peter Cushing. I was playing a policeman who walks into the TARDIS, looking like a police box, and off we went.

We did have a funny thing with the director, Gordon Flemyng, bless him. I've told this story quite often but it's still worth the retelling. Peter and I were introduced to the Daleks, and there's one coming down the ramp towards us. The guy operating it was Bob Jewell. He was one of the first guys with all the lines to communicate with the actors and he was quiety shuffling along inside. Then, all of a sudden, out of this thing came this broad Australian voice saying, "You will be exterminated!"

That was it. Peter and I just disappeared. We were off, giggling, and this Dalek is saying, "Stand still! Da da da!" Gordon got extremely cross. "Stop bloody laughing!" Growling at us, he was. We got slapped wrists for that but it was very funny.

> **"I spent most of my time chasing him. He could shift!"**

Many, many years later, there I was with the Daleks again on the TV series, although filming in Cardiff was very different. You didn't really rehearse that much. You learned the jokes at home and then came in and found out where you were going to sit, stand or walk to... Or run to, in the case of David Tennant. I spent most of my time chasing him. He could shift! He could've beaten Usain Bolt on a good day!

This time round, I shot a Dalek right in the eye. I know that Russell T Davies, who wrote the script, won't mind me saying that was actually my idea. My character, Wilfred, might've been an idiot but I thought, "He'd have some sort of ploy, being an old soldier". And so I thought of a paint gun. That was it. Of course, the paint starts to melt as the Dalek burns it off, and the next thing is — "Zap!" —

Billie Piper appears with a monstrous ray gun or whatever. So I got another of my lines in: "Do you want to swap?"

What the Dalek says in that scene – "My vision is not impaired!" – perhaps we should have stuck a plastic cup or something over the end. That'd've been easier, wouldn't it?

Ingrid Oliver

Actress and comedian
Snogged John Barrowman when he appeared as a guest on Watson & Oliver in 2012

I don't exactly recall when I started watching Doctor Who as I was only a wee lass at the time, but I do remember that my first ever crush was Colin Baker. Incidentally, I also had a massive crush on Michael Ball, so I obviously had a thing about avuncular, tousle-haired blond men. I was quite a geeky girl growing up (I read a fair few comic books) and always preferred brains over brawn. To me, the Doctor was the incarnation of that ideal. I've always thought that if James Bond is the classic archetype of an alpha male then the Doctor is the perfect beta.

"My first ever crush was Colin Baker."

When I got the call from my agent telling me I'd got the part in Doctor Who, I asked him to repeat what he'd just said because I was in complete shock and didn't believe him! After I got off the phone, I spent an hour walking around aimlessly repeating, "Oh my God, oh my God" over and over again. I still don't think it's sunk in.

I was more nervous than I'd been about any previous audition. I decided that the character I was going in for would definitely wear glasses. Now, I've never admitted this before, but as I'm not a glasses-wearer, I borrowed my boyfriend's and wore them at the audition, pretending they were my own and that I needed them to read. Well, it must have worked, because I got the part and the character I played wore them on screen!

Not only that, I even wore a Tom Baker scarf. Now *that* was unbelievably exciting. We filmed a scene in Trafalgar Square and, within hours, hundreds of Doctor Who fans had turned up thanks to the power of Twitter. I looked over to where the crowds had started gathering and saw two chaps wearing exactly the same Doctor-scarf as me. We were not really supposed to encourage photographs, as the powers that be didn't want any spoilers getting out before the show aired, but I couldn't resist having a pic taken between the two of them. It's one of the best photos I own.

John Leeson
Actor
Voice of K-9

Was I ever "behind the sofa" myself back in 1963 when William Hartnell took on the perils of Monochrome Time Travel at the BBC? Quite honestly, I can't remember — but then 50 years distance in time does tend to corrupt the memory banks a bit. Today, celebrating the broadcast half-century of Doctor Who, I have very few fears for the series' continued longevity. My own part in it, as the voice and "soul" of the infuriatingly pedantic K-9, was an accident. Literally.

A director friend knew my background as a relatively flexible actor, and suggested my name to Graham Williams, the series producer across most of the Tom Baker era. Graham's first instinct was to apologise to me that K-9 was only written-in for a single storyline — *The Invisible Enemy* — but he asked me to voice a second part, that of the Virus of the Swarm. This enemy physically looked rather like an oversized prawn that had been kept out of the fridge (in a warm kitchen) for maybe a fortnight too long. I accepted the part(s) — and 35 years later K-9 is still active somewhere in the cosmos, despite a number of efforts to kill him off! Who'd have thought it?

"K-9 is still active somewhere in the cosmos."

The Virus? I guess that particular mollusc has long been binned under health and safety regulations.

Quite rightly, I had been booked as an actor rather than a voiceover artist feeding in from the sidelines. The rehearsals for the first episode found me "acting" by being K-9, running around as the dog on the rehearsal room floor, the physical prop of K-9 being still in preparation at the BBC workshops. But what a gift of a dynamic! I remain convinced that the sparky relationship Tom Baker and I were able to exploit from the rehearsal room floor was crucial to the character's longevity. Admittedly, when the radio-controlled K-9 module caused technical problems in the studio, I suspected that the character's life would be severely time-limited, but no — the concept of the Doctor having a metal dog that knew more than he did caught on!

What is it they say? "Every dog has his day…"? As I write this, K-9 seems to have proved himself fairly indestructible — in the memory, at least!

Sarah Ann Kennedy

Writer, lecturer, voice artist
Starred alongside David Graham, the original Dalek voice, in four series of Peppa Pig

I think Doctor Who is quite inherent to everyone's childhood. A few years ago, when my niece and nephew were about 10, I took them to a Doctor Who museum in Blackpool. Their Doctor was David Tennant, they loved him so much. But they just laughed and laughed when they saw my Doctor: "He's really old. He looks ridiculous."

They were talking about Jon Pertwee. (I'm a lot older than people think.)

"He's really old. He looks ridiculous."

My parents were quite funny about television. We weren't allowed to watch that much, and we didn't even have a colour set until the 1980s, which is comparatively late. So watching telly was quite a big treat. Even though Jon Pertwee's episodes were broadcast in colour, we could only see them in black and white. Funnily enough, in my memory they were always colour.

I was slightly embarrassed by our television. If any of my friends came around to play I'd suggest we do anything else rather than switch it on. But it was quite a big deal being able to watch Doctor Who. It meant that, in school the following week, I could join in with everyone talking about it. That sort of thing was really important.

The episodes I liked the most were the ones set in England, rather than some fictitious, faraway place. Those early 1970s stories, with the Doctor exiled to Earth, were much more frightening to me, because I could almost believe they could happen. I was the youngest child in our family, about five at the time, so I probably shouldn't have been watching it at all. In fact, I rarely did. I remember more about the back of my parents' black sofa than any particular episode, and the patterned yellow carpet I'd much rather look at than the screen.

By the time I was old enough to watch it on my own, the Doctor had regenerated into Tom Baker. I didn't like him so much, he didn't seem real to me. I think I was quite loyal to "the old one", even though the idea of the Doctor changing his appearance was built into the show. It's like pop music. Each new generation laughs at the stuff their parents liked. It's not until you're much older that you start to appreciate it.

My own daughter is a bit young for the show — she's the same age now that I was when I first started watching — but no doubt in a few years' time, she'll have her own Doctor. And no doubt she'll look back and laugh at my niece and nephew and how much they adored silly old, ridiculous-looking David Tennant.

Sophia Myles

Actress
Took Dawn French as her plus one to the Doctor Who series three premiere in Mayfair

I'm going to out myself.

I *was* Mme Du Pompadour and I have got no idea what was going on in *The Girl in the Fireplace*.

No, really. I read the script, I tried to get it. I showed up. I really wanted to understand what was going on at the time — in the moment, it kind of made sense. Then I watched it, and… well I guess

I'm not "science fiction" enough for it. (Let me get this straight: there's a spaceship, and she's from 18th century France, and there are portholes? It's almost too much.) I've watched it a million times. My mum's tried to explain it, my brother has, my boyfriend has…

So I've often found myself trying to bluff my way through talking about this episode; trying to sound like a cool chick who knew what she was doing but I really didn't.

However, I do think the story's really beautiful. To be honest, when I read the script the thing that I fell in love with was the romance and the human connection. I didn't come with any stress on my own shoulders because I had no preconceived ideas about Doctor Who other than that my bro used to watch it. I knew when I was offered the job what a big deal it was. I didn't know what I was walking into but I had full respect for it. Like I said at the time, it felt like jury service, a calling to an institution: "Of course I must do it."

"I didn't know that the Doctor hadn't snogged anyone before."

For many reasons, though, the experience of *The Girl in the Fireplace* was so beautiful to me because I got to work close to where my ancestors lived. They were all from South Wales, and Doctor Who has opened up the whole industry there. I'm in love with the land and I feel very at home so to get to work there was amazing. At the time, you could sense magic was in the air — fireworks going off. It only took us two weeks to shoot but it was the most natural, beautiful process.

Then we recorded the final scene, where the Doctor reads Pompadour's final letter. I was so sad that it was all finished as I read the lines, and I was thinking, "Hang on! What? She died? When did she die? I thought they were supposed to be a match made in heaven?" And I just welled up because it was my last day.

Looking back, I can see why everyone was so excited by this episode. For one thing, I didn't know that the Doctor hadn't snogged anyone before. (That's why they never gave me my own action figure, I bet. No boy wants to play with a girl in a dress. Well, not until they're older.) Sadly, I can't give anything more away because I now know the Doctor's deepest, darkest secrets. I've been in his head.

Christopher H Bidmead

Writer, journalist, former Doctor Who script editor
*Wrote all his scripts for the series on a Vector Graphic
MZ System B computer*

Gosh! We'd just lost Tom. John Nathan-Turner came into my office across the corridor from his in Union House wearing that Cheshire Cat grin. No cigarette curled between his fingers, happily. "We need a new Doctor," he said.

When I say "lost Tom" I refer, of course, to the "mutual consent not to renew his contract after seven years' employment in the role". Contemplating future series without Tom left us feeling like a dog without a bark. The idea that we'd actively let Tom go restored some feeling of control over the situation.

There was an upside. Tom *was* the show, and he knew it. He was wont to "improve" the scripts on the fly in rehearsal, and his ideas for the series and mine occupied opposite poles of the universe. Tom knew Doctor Who and its audience inside out; I was the bright new boy with the bright new ideas. Well, not new. Doctor Who veteran Barry Letts had talked me through the original concepts and I now had what in today's corporate-speak would be called a "vision" of the series: medieval mystery plays meet Adventures Through Science. I took it all very seriously and expected others to do the same. Tom… er… didn't.

> **"I took it all very seriously and expected others to do the same."**

John looked at me across the desk. "New Doctor. Ideas? Can that thing suggest anything?"

He nodded towards my Hewlett-Packard calculator, one of the first able to print alphanumeric characters, and a forerunner to the personal computer

I would buy a month or two later. I'd programmed it to come up with possible names for Doctor Who stories, and it was chattering out titles like Doctor Who and the Casket of Doom, Death and the Doctor, The Rankoid Relation and so forth. Nothing serious there. My little joke.

I reached for a pad of paper and wrote down some names while John fumbled for a cigarette. I worked fast — he was not going to light that damn thing in my office. I slid the paper across the desk to him.

John ran his finger down the list. "Yes, that would work... Yes, he'd be good... Don't think we could afford him..." He flicked his lighter. But the flame stopped midway to the cigarette. "What!?"

He looked up at me with a sneer of disbelief. "We can't use her. Not a woman. She's female."

Mercifully the lighter had clicked shut, the cigarette unlit.

John got up. "He's called 'the Doctor'", he said. "The show, Chris, is called *Doctor* Who." Now he was heading for the door. "I'll see if we can get Peter Davison."

David J Howe

Author, publisher, merchandise collector
Played the voice of Tony the Cyberman in an edition of Saturday Superstore

It's Saturday 18 November, 1967.

The time: around 5.45pm.

I am six years old and cowering outside the living room as the sounds of Doctor Who filter through the door. Inside the room is my younger brother, Alan. He is three years old, and unconcerned that Varga, the terrifying Ice Warrior, has kidnapped Victoria from the humans' base and is using some stolen power packs to defrost the glacier to free his fellow Warriors, who are trapped inside like flies in amber.

I am petrified. I want to watch Doctor Who but the show is giving me nightmares. I steal a glimpse around the door and catch sight of the screen — Varga is hissing in triumph as the other giant aliens are revealed in the ice. Alan rushes at me suddenly, hissing himself — younger brothers have a habit of knowing how to torment their siblings — and I duck away behind the door again. I hear the wail of the end title theme and sigh as I know I have missed an episode…

"I can still remember not watching the second episode."

Well, it shouldn't be so frightening, then!

40-odd years later and I can still remember not watching the second episode of *The Ice Warriors* because it was too much for me. I think that perhaps this was the key moment when I became a fan; terrified and fascinated by the show in equal parts; enthralled by the monsters, by the wonderful Doctor (played at the time by Patrick Troughton), his brave companions Victoria and Jamie, and the crazy whooshing theme tune which has haunted me all my life.

Of course the final irony is that this particular episode is still one of many lost from the BBC's archives… so while I can listen to the soundtrack and see photographs from it, even today I cannot watch Varga release his crew from the ice.

Robin Ince
Writer and performer
Bought Mankind's 1978 cover of the Doctor Who theme on 7" at Supertone in Little Chalfont

Remembering Doctor Who has been a challenge. It was so omnipresent in my childhood life that nothing seems to stand out as it was just always there, a benevolent hostage situation for my mind. There were occasional breaks where I would run around in my pants with a kitchen knife imagining I was Ron Ely and, once, myself and a taller Canadian child would re-enact the life of Steve Austin and Bigfoot, but that was it.

But there is one memory that seems clearer than most…

It was thanks to Doctor Who that I realised a career in special effects was not for me.

Saturday morning kids' TV was the inspiration. Even now, terrestrial weekend children's TV seems a quaint artefact from a previous century. Our morning king was Noel Edmonds, a pasteurised Kenny Everett whose "wackiness" would not contaminate young minds with possible anarchy. A regular feature on his Multi-Coloured Swap Shop — a local papers classified section with added Boney M — would be interviews with the model-making geniuses who took cogs, glue and offcuts and turned them into spaceships.

"I took to using the family tape recorder to make my own sound effects."

After each episode of Doctor Who I would find whatever rusted objects lay in the bit of the garden at the back where rusty stuff was kept and stick the bits together. After half an hour, rather than a rocket or manned asteroid, I just had some scrap that was slightly more ordered than before, a universe that had briefly and pointlessly fought against the entropy. Sometimes I would glue something leftover from an Airfix kit on to a detached pram wheel. If these were space stations then the enemy would have been a mummified nanny played by Wendy Craig.

Once I'd failed at that I took to using the family tape recorder to make my own sound effects. The best of these was the sound of a sponge squelching in my old potty which I created using a sponge and my old potty. Sometimes I would also record the voice of a terrifying robot which sounded like a nuisance call.

Fortunately, all of these tapes were later wiped and re-used to record the audio of The Goodies off the TV, though all you could hear was a child laughing raucously and an occasional squeal from Tim Brooke-Taylor.

By 1981, Tom Baker regenerated and my mind moved on to Alexei Sayle, Rik Mayall and the burgeoning idea that it might be fun to shout on stage for a living…

And eventually, that's just what I did.

Clayton Hickman

Writer, designer, talking head
Had a medical procedure in Torchwood named after him

It's 2005. Doctor Who has just returned to amazing ratings and critical acclaim, and I'm the editor of Doctor Who Magazine. Which is nice. The first episodes of the second series, starring David Tennant, are already filming, but I'm stuck in Tunbridge Wells doing editory things. Then I get a phone call. It's not the new Doctor — not today, anyway — but there's a very familiar voice at the end of the line.

"It's my first day on Doctor Who tomorrow," says Elisabeth Sladen. "Are you busy? 'Cos everyone's lovely, but I could really do with a familiar face there. But only if you're free, if it's not too much faff…"

Not only was it not too much faff, it was also the most flattering invitation to a momentous day's filming on my favourite TV show. It was also incredibly surreal — I was a familiar face to Sarah Jane Smith? What about Benton? Or Brendan? Perhaps I was the new Aunt Lavinia?

"I was a familiar face to Sarah Jane Smith? What about Benton?"

Anyway, there I was, the next day, Tuesday 23 August, standing in the sunshine outside Fitzalan High School in Cardiff, watching Sarah Jane and Doctor Who running away from an explosion. My familiar face was too busy grinning to be of much use, but then Lis had no need to worry.

"Did that look okay, that old woman hobbling along there?" she asked.

"It looked like a million dollars, and so did you, so shut up and stop fretting, Sladen!" She doesn't know, and neither do I, that this is just the first day of what will become a whole new chapter in her career.

Later, after more running and a quick interview, Lis is done for the day. We head back to the hotel where she makes a second, rather more odd request. She has an escape plan worthy of Sarah herself — not from the show, which she's loving, but from her hotel suite. It's next door to the lift shaft, which is banging away all hours, keeping her awake and probably sounds a bit like that compost grinder in *The Seeds of Doom*. Would I possibly help shift her stuff to her new room?

Of course I would! So Lis and I, and a bewildered hotel porter with a big trolley, proceed to transport what appear to be all of Lis's worldly goods and possessions. My face was deemed familiar enough to qualify for the guardianship of several drawers' worth of drawers and assorted dainties. The porter is totally mystified by our cackling, but with Sarah Jane's bras over my shoulder I've reached new heights of surrealness.

I loved Lis Sladen — and that day is one of the many, many reasons why.

Murray Gold

Dramatist, musician and composer
Bought The Claws of Axos *on DVD just because he liked the incidental music*

I watched Doctor Who every Saturday night without fail from around 1974 till about 1980.

It's pretty easy to date my memories because as far as I know, the show wasn't repeated, and I've not watched the classic series since, so anything I know about early episodes is from first broadcast. And I guess I was pretty shocked to find that, say, *The Green Death* was transmitted in 1973. So I was four, but I remember so much about it. That's kind of insightful to know how much you remember at that age.

"I loved the repulsive stuff." So, yeah, I went to Portchester Northern County Infant/Junior School back in the day. I was friends with a guy there called Gavin Fuller. I guess we were both a bit geeky although I'm not sure we knew it. I used to go round his house and he'd have the Target novels and we'd talk about them a lot.

He ended up winning Mastermind and I think one of his rounds was on Doctor Who. Now he reviews the show for The Daily Telegraph, and I became the composer on the show, so it all went in sort of a circle.

I guess I was a Philip Hinchcliffe era guy. I loved the repulsive stuff. The body horror. Like Noah's hand in *The Ark in Space*. I don't want to go back and watch it because it won't be scary anymore. I prefer it to be a memory. I'm not a nostalgia junky. Once upon a time nostalgia was treated as an illness. Excessive fondness for the past, etc.

And since my own involvement with the show, there have just been so many days and moments I will treasure. The lovely speech at the end of *Love & Monsters*: "The world is so much stranger than that. It's so much darker. And so much madder. And so much better." Rose and chips. Rose on the beach. The *whole* of the last two episodes of the 2010 series. On a personal note, the Proms and Melbourne. And the lovely, talented, generous people I've met along the way. It's the best show in the world, and I'm not opening that up to the floor for debate.

Chris Chibnall
Writer and producer
Was given a gingerbread man prop from The Christmas Invasion *for his tree*

We stand in front of the wooden blue door.

"Are you ready?" I ask my son. He nods. Cal is four and well versed in that door. He has been anticipating this for months. Now his eyes are fixed, staring up at the illuminated sign that says "Police Public Call Box".

I push the door gently and hold it open for him. He walks through, under my arm.

He doesn't gasp or go "Wow!" because what's inside is exactly what he expects to be there. Domed walls of roundels. A console with a huge column in the centre. Wires and coral-like structures. All lit up.

"Can I touch it?" he asks. I tell him I think so, but to be careful. We don't want to break it. Or accidentally take off.

Of course, what he really wants to do is take off.

He takes his time, walks slowly round the entire console. He pumps the pump. He picks up the Trimphone and listens in. No-one there.

I lift him up on to the seat where the Doctor sat with Rose, teasing Mickey, before falling into a parallel universe. But he doesn't want to sit there long. He wants to explore. Because for these few minutes, he has the TARDIS all to himself.

He looks up and around. To me, this is a big construction. Even on my third visit, this is like no set I've ever seen. What must it be like when you're around three feet tall?

He doesn't mention the absence of a fourth wall; that you look out into a vast, dark, black studio where, somewhere out front, Brian Minchin, brilliant script editor, is watching us to make sure we don't break the TARDIS.

> **"For these few minutes, my son has the TARDIS all to himself."**

Does he think this is happening for real? Does he know it's television? What's his relationship to today? I daren't ask. I don't want to spoil it.

I step down off the set, leaving him alone up there. I walk over to Brian, my wife Madeline, and our younger son, all but a baby, who'll never remember he was also on the TARDIS. We watch and take pictures.

Then Cal looks out for a second, sees us there. He calls me over. And I think, "Oh no! It's spoiled now. He's recognised the artifice."

I walk over and stand underneath the raised console, lower than him. He looks down at me and explains: "When the Doctor's in here, the walls come together and this bit closes up".

I nod. Yes.

He heads off again. And I watch this small figure exploring, craning his neck backwards, to look up, right to the top. Lost in wonder at the TARDIS. Just like I've always been.

Sophie Aldred

Actress, played the Doctor's companion Ace
Wanted to be Sarah Jane Smith when she grew up

Like all good British children, I was brought up on a healthy diet of Blue Peter, Basil Brush and Doctor Who.

I used to watch Doctor Who through a crack in the door and make my younger brother watch it with his face in a cushion on the sofa so he could see the scary bits and tell me afterwards. But I do remember being terrified. In fact, I was so terrified of the Cybermen when I was little that my Mum stopped me watching it for a while because I would have nightmares.

Little did I know that, 20 years later, I'd be slaying them with a cata-pult and gold coins on a gantry during the story *Silver Nemesis*.

In rehearsal the director said to me, "Oh, you're alright with heights aren't you, Sophie?" When we got there — it was where the O2 Arena is now — I walked into this massive arching hangar and there was this tiny little platform way, way up high. Hundreds of feet, maybe, I dunno.

Luckily for me, all of the Cybermen — or, rather, the men inside the Cybermen suits — were very tall, very handsome male models. (Gary Downie, the programme's somewhat camp floor manager, had decided this would be a good way forward, to have a bit of eye-candy around.) Not only that, they were all incredibly intel-ligent, nice blokes and so I was slightly distracted by having a wonderful conversation with the guy I was then going to kill. I really didn't notice the height while I was up there, which was a good thing!

John Nathan-Turner, the producer, used to put on these weekends at Llangollen. They were called Travellers in Time and people used to pay to go. The idea was you'd have a meal in the restaurant with us — me and Sylvester or whoever in the evening — and then, the following day, we'd all go on the steam railway together. After that, we'd take a canal boat over the highest viaduct in Christendom, until, finally — the treat of all treats! — a visit to the Dapol model factory. There'd be a chance to make your own Doctor Who figure, rattling Daleks and Cybermen off the production line. All the fans would be absolutely overjoyed. And so would I.

> ## "Luckily for me, all of the Cybermen were very tall, handsome, male models."

And now, here I am, yet another 20 years on. As I sit at my kitchen table, I'm looking up at my window sill on which sits a plastic Dapol figure of a Cyberman, a Sylvester Doctor and an Ace. I think about that little girl who watched Jon Pertwee running away from giant maggots in *The Green Death*. I reckon, if somebody had told that little girl she was one day going to have a little plastic doll of herself — looking quite cool, although not much like her, but with this great jacket with badges all over it — I don't think she'd have been terrified at all.

I think she'd have been amazed.

Jon Peake

Editor-in-chief of TV Choice and Total TV Guide
Bought a table on eBay which was handmade by Mary Tamm's father

For years, the one thing that truly frightened me was the thought of shop mannequins coming to life.

Why? The Doctor Who story *Spearhead from Space*.

For the longest time, I had only the vaguest jigsaw memory of the series, but no idea how it all fitted together and which part was which. So when a friend offered to lend me the DVD I had to see it. But would I be able to watch it on my own?

It turned out that I would.

Was it still scary? Well no — I'm 46 — but, truthfully, it's not lost its capacity to make one feel just a little bit uncomfortable. As a child

I was totally spooked. The story is rather still and menacing, and the very idea that a tailor's dummy should come to life and wish harm upon you was all too much.

One of my grandparents ran a pub. Behind the frosted glass doors of the billiard room were rounded shapes which were silent and didn't seem to move much. They were clearly Autons. I couldn't even look in that door's direction.

Another grandparent lived on the edge of a common, on which was a little groundsman's cottage, which was unfortunately a little *too* close for comfort in aspect to the one the Autons called upon. When we went into the common we had to circumnavigate it. It was simply not worth the risk.

Like all early Doctor Who stories, though, *Spearhead* is kind of stagey in places. Also, I can now see that the rather rudimentary mannequin masks the actors wore aren't really anything to fear. But the blank, no-eyed stare, bald pate and habit of bursting out of shop windows on a mission to kill (in Ealing, fact fans) haven't lost any of their thrill. And the scene in Madame Tussaud's is all my nightmares made flesh — okay, plastic.

Thanks to the DVD extras, I did discover some interesting facts about this story, the main one being that it was Jon Pertwee's first outing as the Doctor. Which means I was peeking out from behind the sofa as far back as 1970. Where I'd previously scoffed at the notion that there would be British military figures on show in Tussauds, a look at a late 1950s guide to the museum indicates they were out in force. I'm not entirely sure that this was still the case as the 1970s dawned, however.

> **"The scene in Madame Tussaud's is all my nightmares made flesh."**

Like a lot of people, I imagine, I've often confused this story with its sequel, *Terror of the Autons*. I'm still unsure which story has the evil rubber doll lying in wait behind the curtain to pop off that old duffer, but it doesn't matter. Of all the stories I've seen it's still the one I like the most, the one that never fails to make the hairs on the back of my neck stand on end.

Tom Pearcy

Former farmer
Created York Maze, Europe's largest maize maze, in the shape of a Dalek, in 2013

I'd first seen a maize maze in America. I was a farmer at the time so I thought I'd go and have a bit of a nosey. It was like Field of Dreams — "If you build it, he will come" — and there was a bloke sat at the edge with a table and a money box, charging people a couple of dollars to get in.

I thought, "I could have a go at that." All told now, I've been doing it for 10 years. For Doctor Who's anniversary year, the York Maze design featured the biggest image of a Dalek ever created, over 300 metres long, cut out of an 18 acre field of over one million living maize plants.

I've always tried to create something with a very strong aerial image first and foremost, rather than a really difficult maze. We've found that kids don't like to be thwarted at the first turn. Mine are made to be relatively easy but large scale, so that it's time consuming to explore. Unless you're five hundred feet above it, however, it's very difficult to get any concept of the image you're walking around in.

"William Hartnell's face was quite a struggle."

We played around designing a maze with just a TARDIS or a Dalek, but I wanted to cover the 50-year span of Doctor Who. Trying to get William Hartnell's face to work was quite a struggle. It was a bit easier with Matt Smith as his facial features are quite strong. There's only a certain amount we can do with a small tractor and a cultivator in a field, though. It can all be a bit tricky, but it's fun.

To launch our Doctor Who maze, we managed to persuade Colin Baker to come down for the day, and he was a pleasure to work with. We hid a TARDIS somewhere in the maze, too, as a little surprise for people. But, as a Doctor Who fan, and a bit of a Dalek devotee, for me it was all just a great excuse to buy my own life-sized Dalek. The missus was horrified when I pitched up with it in the van. At the minute, my seven-year-old son is badgering me to let him get in and drive it. Everyone loves a Dalek, don't they?

Adam Roberts

Academic, critic, author
Wrote a Doctor Who-themed parody of Lynn Truss's Eats, Shoots and Leaves under a thinly-veiled pseudonym

Being born halfway through the 1960s meant my first Doctor was the incomparable Jon Pertwee. I was five when he took the role and nine when he stopped; the perfect age-range for a kid's first Who-crush. Ever since then I find myself measuring the accuracy or otherwise of an actor's Doctoricity against the template of Pertwee: his large-featured, seamed, old-man face topped off, improbably enough, with a Brigitte Bardot hair-do; all those crushed velvet jackets and chantilly cuffs; that unashamedly patrician manner.

> **"The perfect age-range for a kid's first Who-crush."**

Given that so many of the actors playing the role have had ditchwater surnames — all those Macs and Eccs and Smiths and not one but *two* Bakers — it is an added glory that Pertwee's name is so wonderfully odd, comprising as it does a first syllable most often paired with the word *buttocks* and a, frankly, urinous second. A nine-year-old boy relishes these sorts of things. In fact, Pertwee's family were of French-Huguenot provenance and my adult self laments that he didn't revert to the original, full, continental "Jon de Perthuis de Laillevault" as his stage name. What splendour could have been!

So, yes: it's always been Pertwee for me. I believe the overarching message of the Pertwee years was that "men may go shooting off into outer space, but it's really their *inner* space that matters most". You don't agree? Hey, you needn't take my word for it. Those are the *exact* words used, in a badly-drawn Pertweevian endorsement, on the back cover of Sarah Charles's Baking Your Cake & Eating It: 100 Baking Recipes (Co-op Books 1973).

And if that essential piece of Doctor Who memorabilia has taught me anything, it is this: in one illustrator's eyes, the Third Doctor had the head of Jon Pertwee but the hands of a much larger Afro-Caribbean man. And he liked cake.

He really liked cake.

Neil Gaiman

Graphic novelist and writer
Won the Ray Bradbury Award for his Doctor Who episode, The Doctor's Wife

Here's how I became a Doctor Who fan.

Do you remember those free bottles of milk they gave out at nursery school (at least until Mrs Thatcher took them away)? You'd drink them with a straw until you got down to the last inch, then you'd blow down to create bubbles. In Mrs Pepper's class, in Purbrook, the kids did something far more interesting. They bent the straws over and pushed them around like Daleks: "I will exterminate you".

Now the milk was delicious but *this*, I thought, was fascinating: "I don't know what it is but I have to find out."

Here's a confession. The Daleks excited me but they didn't frighten me. When I saw the bright colour cover of The Dalek World annual in 1966, sitting on a shelf at WHSmiths, I begged my parents for a copy. I learned so many things, like the fact that Daleks can't see the colour red. (Odd, especially as there seemed to be so many red ones. Perhaps they thought they were invisible.) I still have it now, although no longer with the cover.

So if you were wondering why there are three pages of "fan fiction" by me in The Brilliant Book of Doctor Who, it's because I wanted to recreate that experience; that cool Christmas morning when you'd find the annual in your stocking. (Although your stocking wouldn't be big enough for an annual unless you had elephantisis, I suspect.)

"Doctor Who is like an inoculation of fear."

My strongest memory of Doctor Who may well be the first time I watched it, aged four, round at my grandparents' house. I was frightened of the Zarbi, giant ants the size of men who, I'm certain, could eat you. There was a shared children's knowledge that monsters could look through and come out of the television, that it was their window. But did we run and hide out of the room? No, because then it would be over. We hid behind the sofa because it was a place you could still watch from. It was a controlled space.

If I have one regret, it's that I wish there had been a scary monster in *The Doctor's Wife*. Yes, there was the bad Ood but, looking back, there's no one single moment that would have sent kids scurrying away in terror. If there's one thing that could tempt me back it would be the chance to create a monster to do that.

People ask, "Why do you want to scare kids?" yet they forget that kids like being scared. We have to learn fear to survive. Doctor Who is like an inoculation of fear. A small dose while you're young. It reminds me of the Greek poisoners, who would take the tiniest draughts of poison over time, to build up their immunity, then sit down to take a drink with their enemies. They would survive.

Or is that homeopathy?

The truth is: there's nothing that you can do on screen or in books that will be as frightening to a child as the shadow of a dressing gown hanging on a door, or a noise from behind the closed doors of a wardrobe. Being scared of Doctor Who is like being scared of the ghost train at the fair. You still know, after the spiders and skeletons and cobwebs and creeps, that you will come out at the end. There will be daylight again.

Saul Nassé

BBC Learning controller
Was executive producer of BBC Choice's Doctor Who week in 1998

It was 1973, I was eight and my family had moved from the city of Apollo-era Mission Control, Houston, Texas to Bedford, Bedfordshire, where the most exciting thing happening was the manufacture of Toblerone. For me, America had been McDonald's, Disneyland and air conditioning. Britain was sausage in batter, the waltzer and hot water bottles.

But one thing was so much better: the television. Blue Peter, Jackanory, The Clangers and my new-found favourite, Tomorrow's World, with Raymond Baxter. I'd also seen bits of something called Doctor Who, but it was confusing. Sometimes there were three Doctor Whos, other times only one, plus loads of maggots.

"My mother said we all must watch it."

But then a new Doctor Who season was starting, and my mother said we all must watch it. It turned out it wasn't just me that was new to Who, there was also a spirited young journalist called Sarah Jane Smith who was the perfect companion in this exciting world. And *how* exciting. A man from the army, disappearing scientists, medieval warriors and time travel.

But most of all there was Linx. He had three fingers on each hand, silver armour and a pretty scary voice. What could he possibly be? And, most importantly, what was under that domed shaped helmet? Why did he never take it off? If he only had three fingers he probably didn't look much like my dad. Maybe he was like Herman Munster or one of the hairy beasts from Where the Wild Things Are?

Then suddenly, quite without warning, Linx took his helmet off. We all screamed. His head was exactly the same shape as his helmet, and quite the most revolting thing we had ever seen. The end credits boomed in and I was hooked.

Tomorrow's World would go on to be the show I executive produced 25 years later, but this thing — this Doctor Who — was amazing and I would love it for ever.

Jonathan Morris
Writer
As a child, slept beside a Doctor Who mural hand-painted by his mum and sister

There's nothing quite as exciting as getting a letter from the BBC. They come in white envelopes with a red "BBC" postmark. Those three consonants, B, B and C, summon up so many childhood associations, it's almost like getting a letter from Tucker Jenkins himself; from Posh Paws; from Rod Hull and Emu; from Frank Spencer, Brian Cant and Larry Grayson all rolled into one.

The letter I received from the BBC in 1999 wasn't from any of these people. It was from the editor of BBC Books. A few months earlier, I'd sent in a proposal for a Doctor Who novel. The editor had written back with half a dozen pages of suggestions on how it might be improved — suggestions to be implemented in a re-submitted proposal. So I implemented the suggestions, re-submitted, and then waited, trying not to get my hopes up, for the letter from the BBC.

"At last, I'd be making my own contribution to the legend."

And here it was. Inside, there was a letter from the editor. They liked the new proposal and wanted to commission me to write the entire novel. A contract would be with me shortly, no doubt courtesy of another white BBC envelope.

It was the most exciting moment. At last I would be doing the one thing I had always dreamed of — writing Doctor Who stories. Ever since I was a six-year-old precociously stapling together the pages of my 12-page novella, Docter Who and the Conquer of Time. Ever since I was a nauseating adolescent of 15 sending the show's script editor a storyline about the Doctor defeating alien body-snatchers in a space hospital. At last, I'd be making my own contribution to the legend — small, insignificant and non-canonical as it would no doubt be.

Then the fear hit me. Within seconds I was convinced I was about to write the worst Doctor Who novel ever. I would be widely derided. I would be mocked on the internet. All my ambitions would be shown to be delusions.

I wouldn't be able to do it.

But fear of failure is the secret of success. It just meant I had to try harder. So I wrote like I had never written before or have ever written since. So many hours, so much painstaking care. And I absolutely adored every second of it.

That feeling is just as strong now, whenever I get asked to write something. It never goes away and it never diminishes. It does, however, become addictive.

Stuart Flanagan

Resident doctor on BBC Radio 1's Surgery
Once travelled exactly 100 miles to meet Tom Baker

It's Christmas morning and I'm four years old. Life really doesn't get any more exciting than this. Mum has led me from my bedroom, hands across my eyes. I stand on the threshold of the front room, anticipating a cavalcade of glitter, lights and treasures. But most of all, more than anything else, I want to see my hero today: that mad man in a blue box.

For once, all my dreams come true — Santa has fixed it for me! There he is, that intrepid explorer of the galaxies, with his dazzling grin, impossibly long scarf, trusty sonic screwdriver and mass of curls. And he's 10 inches tall with the face of Gareth Hunt.

I've got my hands on my most prized possession — a Doctor Who action figure. He's arrived with his glorious, revolving door TARDIS and friction drive K-9, on the brink of a thousand new adventures in my bedroom, bathroom, or back garden.

Years later as a geeky fanboy I'd curse that fact that the boxes from these rare and precious Denys Fisher toys were chucked out, mourn the parts that had snapped off, and stare broken-heartedly at the unhinged TARDIS doors. But as time goes on, I've realised that these scars are the memories of happy days playing joyously with my hero, battling injustice and fear with wide grins on both our faces. They're reminders of the Sunday afternoons my granddad spent re-attaching the Doctor's dislocated limbs, so he could journey off again with me on another terrifying escapade.

> **"He's 10 inches tall with the face of Gareth Hunt."**

Those loving repairs mean my Doctor Who figure is still with me now. His hat is a little battered, and the scarf a little frayed at the edges, but he's ready for adventure still. From time to time I'll take him down from the shelf, and recreate those endless summers when he battled Darth Vader or Skeletor. After all… there's no point in being grown up if you can't be childish sometimes.

Dave Chapman

Actor and puppeteer
Scratch-built a 30cm-high Dalek as an eight-year-old

Very early on a freezing cold, rainy Monday morning in February 1999 I drove out of West London headed for Pinewood in Buckinghamshire. Comic Relief had been kindly donated studio space for free to shoot their Doctor Who spoof, The Curse of Fatal Death. I soon realised that "free" meant "unheated" and the sub-zero temperatures of M Stage would require me to keep my coat on for the rest of the week.

My tasks were to play the lead Dalek, help co-ordinate the supporting artists who were also playing Daleks, and read in the Daleks' lines on set to assist the actors with timing. At the time, Doctor Who had been off our screens for a few years. For that reason, a lot of the Daleks, all of the interior of the TARDIS and a few other props were actually being lent to the shoot by fans who, as a thank-you, were allowed to visit the set and see us working.

I had always imagined that Daleks had a little steering wheel and gear box, and pedals, a bit like a bumper car — so I was quite surprised when first getting inside one to find they were actually more like Fred Flintstone's car, and the engine consisted only of my feet.

It didn't take long for everyone to conclude that, for rehearsals, the Dalek's top half should be left off, so the performer inside could be heard. Therefore, for most of the week, I found myself booming out guide dialogue, sat in half a Dalek, while surrounded by some of the finest actors in the business. Rowan Atkinson, Jonathan Pryce, Richard E Grant, and half a dozen hovering Who obsessives. With an audience like that, it was altogether quite a surreal experience.

> **"I had always imagined that Daleks had a little steering wheel and gear box."**

As a result of my screeching, the producers asked me to provide some of the Dalek voices to be used on the show, alongside the contributions of the legendary Roy Skelton. So, in a post-production facility in Camden a few weeks later, I spent a morning dubbing the action. I can't deny that, secretly,

I was really pleased to be standing in a sound booth shouting, "Exter-min-ate!" and remembering back to childhood when that single word, in that strange voice, scared the living daylights out of me.

David Quantick

Journalist and writer
Was profoundly affected by the sight of Alpha Centauri in The Curse of Peladon

I have always loved Doctor Who. And I *mean* always — my dad still maintains I saw the first episode (presumably I was hiding behind my playpen at the time). So when I was commissioned to write an episode of the audio series I was insanely delighted. I'd asked my agent to investigate the possibility when the programme was off the air — by the time the answer came back "yes" it'd long since triumphantly returned to TV.

> **"I learned that there's a whole world of Who people out there."**

They gave me Sylvester McCoy— the most underrated Doctor Who, if you ask me; a man born out of time — and Sophie Aldred, his lovely assistant. They even invited me to the recording of the resulting episode, *The Dark Husband*. Spending the day with the cast, and listening to their superb Doctor Who stories was a real eye-opener (such as the one about the Doctor who famously hated the Daleks because he thought they upstaged him). I had my photo taken with the cast, and shared a glass of wine in the boozer after the story was "in the can". I learned that there's a whole world of Who people out there — nearly 50 years of Doctors and companions who all meet at conventions and launches — and their pride in being part of the show is very apparent.

Mind you, a few months later, when I asked my agent to investigate the possibility of writing another audio story, the producers asked me to send in a CV of the work I'd done in the past. I think they'd actually erased me from their minds! Never mind. I was very happy to briefly be a very small part of the Who community.

If that sounds modest, it's not meant to be — thanks to the likes of Russell T Davies, Doctor Who's ongoing history is such a huge and powerful thing it makes Star Wars look like a wasp's tear in an egg cup.

Talking of which, shortly after my audio had been recorded, I met Russell at a BBC do and he knew what I'd done. "Ah!" he said. "A closet Doctor Who fan!"

Aren't we all? Although there's nothing secret about it. Doctor Who's been part of my life from crib to pub — from Hartnell to Capaldi — and I hope it continues to be for a very, very long time.

Richard Coles

Broadcaster, Church of England priest, former pianist with The Communards
As a child, really, really loved the Master

We have a family legend. One time, my dad was driving down to Norfolk where we spent all our holidays. The car broke down, gushing steam just outside of Wisbech, and my brother said, "Dad, you need to get your sonic screwdriver."

My dad had a sonic screwdriver!

Well, he was always *fixing* things with it.

I used to get him to switch on the TV when Doctor Who was on. I couldn't do it myself, I was so frightened of Cybermen, with their little eyeholes and the strange kind of galvanised bucket head. Your favourite Doctor is always the one that hits you when you "come online", as it were, and for me it was always Patrick Troughton. Even if the monsters were pretty rubbish in his day.

"My dad had a sonic screwdriver!"

In those days I had a Dalek costume and there is in existence, somewhere, a Super 8 film of me riding my bike in it. It had a big, plastic skirt and a head-piece, and I remember buying it from Curry's in Kettering. That would have been about 1970 I should think. Me, on my Raleigh bike, going round and round the front yard, in my Dalek costume: this stupid boy.

But it wasn't my favourite piece of merchandise. That honour belonged to my TARDIS Commander badge. I have a vivid image in my mind of me in my lovely blue anorak. I would always wear it with my TARDIS Commander badge, big and white (about the size of a soup plate as I remember it), and with a picture of the TARDIS on it.

I was absolutely fascinated by how the TARDIS worked. I had a book with all the pseudo-science about it. I needed to know. After all, my dad had a sonic screwdriver!

Actually, what I realised, years later, was that what he called his sonic screwdriver was a pressure gauge for the car tyre. But for a while I really did believe it was a sonic screwdriver and that my dad had all sorts of powers.

Nicholas Parsons

Actor, TV and radio presenter
Played the Rev. Mr Wainwright in The Curse of Fenric

A favourite memory of Doctor Who was filming in Hawkhurst, Kent, using a beautiful old church as the rectory in the story. On location, there was a mobile wardrobe van, where we changed, and no dressing room, so I was moving about the village quite a lot in costume. On one occasion I was standing beside the lychgate to the church when a lady came up and said, "Oh, Vicar, I am so pleased to have caught you. Can I come and talk to you about a christening?"

"At one time my teeth were actually chattering during a take."

I replied that she could but I doubted very much if I could help. She looked at me for a moment and then recognition dawned and she was overcome with confusion.

"Oh, I am so sorry, you're not... I mean you are... Oh dear... I recognise you... you're Nicolson Parkinson... I mean... The Century man... Oh, I do feel a fool!"

I quickly reassured her that she was not foolish and she had flattered me by mistaking me for the genuine article. I took her to the real vicar, who was inside the church and who had been very kind to lend me some of his vestments to wear.

The filming was all done on location and one sequence was shot in an army training camp in Crowborough, Sussex. These were the final scenes in the finished programme but were recorded much earlier in the production.

It was April and bitterly cold and the snow that had been missing all winter suddenly arrived. It soon melted and the place was a quagmire. The film crew and technicians were wrapped in warm overcoats and balaclavas. The good Doctor, his assistant Ace and the Rev. Mr. Wainwright were, of course, in thin summer clothes. I was literally blue with cold. At one time my teeth were actually chattering during a take, and we had to break the filming to thaw us out over a Primus stove in the army huts.

The rain, snow and slushy ground gave considerable atmosphere to the scene, but when I was overcome by the monstrous Haemovores and trampled to death in the mud, I did not have to fake anything: I was in genuine distress as I lay in the squelchy mire.

Apparently, it's one of the most popular stories with the fans!

Graham Duff

Writer, actor and producer
Smuggled lines from The Caves Of Androzani *into his scripts for comedy series,* Ideal

I stood on a hilltop with my parents and sisters surveying the raw majesty of the Lancashire countryside. Faced with such breathtaking natural beauty, there was only one question I needed to ask: "Will we be back home in time for Doctor Who?" Mum and Dad both assured me I had nothing to worry about.

At the age of eight my whole life revolved around Doctor Who and had done for as long as I could remember. The instant an episode finished, I would spend the remainder of the weekend drawing all the exciting bits. At school on Monday, Sean Connell and I would discuss the episode in minute detail. We'd do much the same thing throughout Tuesday and Wednesday too. Then, come Thursday, we'd start predicting what might happen in the next episode. Actually missing an episode was as unthinkable as eating a salad.

Travelling home in the Austin 1100, I asked Dad if he was absolutely certain we'd be back for the appointed time. When he gave an apologetic shrug and uttered those deathly words — "Maybe not…" — I realised the true horror of the situation; I was going to miss episode four of *The Mutants*! I tried to hide my hot tears from my sisters, all of whom seemed a little shaken by the news themselves. I was inconsolable for the remainder of the journey.

"Actually missing an episode was as unthinkable as eating a salad."

Inevitably, on Monday morning, Sean Connell informed me that I had missed "one of the coolest episodes ever". I had suspected as much. Sean explained that not only had there been an incredible laser battle sequence, but Jo Grant had actually taken her top off.

In these days of iPlayer and BitTorrent, it's hard to imagine a time when, if you missed a programme, it simply dematerialised into the ether. *The Mutants* would not be released on video for over 30 years. And having finally watched episode four, I have to confess, Sean Connell was right. It really is one of the coolest episodes ever.

When the Doctor enters the heart of the radioactive caves and steals a crystal from a spectral statue, for nearly two minutes not a word is spoken. Instead, the screen is ablaze with multicoloured patterns and bursts of lightning as Tristram Carey's dizzying electronic score oscillates on the soundtrack.

It is tense, experimental, narratively abstract and deeply psychedelic. Like nothing else I've ever seen on TV. It's so good in fact, that I was only marginally disappointed when Jo Grant kept her top on.

Stephen Gallagher

Screenwriter and novelist
Wrote his Doctor Who stories while working in Granada TV's presentation department

During the making of *Terminus* I spent a couple of days at Ealing Studios, hanging out with Mark Strickson and Janet Fielding for the filming of the show's 16mm inserts. For them it was a lot of crawling-around-in-ventilator-shafts stuff. The art department had opened up one of the studio tanks — drained, of course — in order to construct a set over different levels. Mixing film and video was standard practice back then. It always looked odd, but everyone accepted it as a necessary convention because TV studio cameras weren't practical for location shooting.

> **"Mark Strickson would try to freak Janet Fielding out."**

Our scenes could have been shot just as effectively in the main studio but dramas needing film inserts were given an extra day on the schedule, so committing them to film was a neat dodge to secure extra production time. The director was Mary Ridge and the film cameraman was Remi Adefarasin, who went on to become a DP in features and high-end American TV; that's his work in Elizabeth and Band Of Brothers.

A writer in a TV studio is like a visitor to a factory floor. A film crew tends to be a more compact, more sociable unit, and it was an enjoyable couple of days. There was a lot of banter with the hard work. Mark Strickson would try to freak Janet Fielding out, which was pretty much impossible. At some point in the day, a trolley came around with tea and cakes. Very BBC, very old-school, very civilised! Mark took a slice of jam roll — like a Swiss Roll, round with a red swirl — and held it up.

"You know what we called these at school?" he said. "Dead baby's arm."

Most of my memories of being on Doctor Who sets involve haste, pressure, conflict, and me desperately trying to scoot out of everybody's way. But that's why this one stands out for me.

Mark Littlewood

Director General of the Institute of Economic Affairs
Almost bought the Fifth Doctor's costume at a Bonham's auction in 2007

The stage of my young love when I was most excited about Doctor Who was probably the arrival of Peter Davison. I was born in 1972 so, as far as I was concerned, Tom Baker really was the Doctor. Although I was conscious there were three predecessors I didn't actually think they would ever change him. So this new Doctor arriving when I was nine years old was absolutely revolutionary to me. For the final episode of *Logopolis*, I put my audio cassette recorder next to the television set and taped it.

I never imagined that I'd live to be old enough to hear Paddy Kingsland's music from that story played at the Royal Albert Hall in the Doctor Who proms. Who would have believed it?

Of course, they then switched the series from Saturdays to weekdays, and it was on twice a week — fantastic news! The idea that you would have to wait either only 24 hours or six days rather than seven was hugely exciting. I was too dumb to realise that this meant the season would be over in just 13 weeks rather than spread over 26.

> **"The new Doctor arriving when I was nine was absolutely revolutionary."**

So *Castrovalva* was a new horizon in Doctor Who for me. It gave credence to the belief that the programme would be around forever. Davison was my favourite Doctor by far. That was when I became absolutely immersed in the series and started collecting everything.

Now I own every extant minute of Doctor Who that's been released on DVD. They are, naturally, arranged in transmission order (with the Lost in Time box set sandwiched between Hartnell and Troughton). I think my girlfriend would attest that the only thing I am remotely tidy with around the house is the order of my Doctor Who DVDs. Everything else in my flat is a mess. These things are very important, though. You have to have a proper system.

Al Murray

Comedian
Asked Peter Davison to reverse the polarity of his robot dog, Ramrod, on TV

I'll get this out of the way: I'm a Tom Baker boy. Some of my hottest memories of telly as a kid are the Fourth Doctor. And the hottest memory of the lot is this: *Pyramids of Mars* — the mummies, Sutekh, the gothic setting. It's scarf-wearing, jelly-baby loving, curly-haired Doctor Who in its pomp.

But the bit that stuck with me — and this is just how the child in me remembers it, so I might get some of it wrong — is when Sarah Jane said words to the effect of, "Well why bother stopping Sutekh? The world didn't end. I'm from 1980. Who cares?" So the Doctor starts up the TARDIS and takes her to 1980. They open the doors...

> **"Scarf-wearing, jelly-baby loving, curly-haired Doctor Who in its pomp."**

And the world is a barren, blasted wasteland. The Doctor says, "See? We have to do something."

It's a fabulous moment that, for me, stands alongside the famous "Have I the right?" moment in *Genesis of the Daleks*. However...

A few summers ago I met Steven Moffat. Ludicrously over-excited, I gushed about how brilliant I thought the show had been under his helm, how I'd got my kids into it, how I hoped they were getting the same kind of hot telly memories as I had all those years ago. And — because, I am sure, he was interested in everything I was telling him — I went on to tell him about my *Pyramids of Mars* moment. And he said, "Yes, I remember, a great moment, and all the better because it's all so obviously filler."

Filler!? I spluttered and gasped. "Yes," he said, with his masterly writer's authority. "Filler."

And yet, who cares? If the filler is that good, what must the content be like?

Louise Mensch

Author and former Conservative party MP
*Disappointed with her given name, demanded to be
called Romana as a child*

Born in 1971, I grew up with two of the great, classic sci-fi series in the shape of Blake's 7 and Doctor Who. And I was therefore lucky enough to enjoy Tom Baker, *the* classic Doctor. It seems strange that out of hundreds of episodes watched, I can't pick out a particularly memorable scene (unlike the final episode of Blake's 7, which scarred me for life). Rather, my memories are of general impressions; suspense, fear... all the good stuff they cut out of kids' programming these days.

The importance of the theme music and the accompanying title sequence in Doctor Who cannot be overstated. The tunnel suggested infinity — death, even — a passage from this world to the next; the way it swirled and spun, and the TARDIS tossed violently within it, made you as a watching child feel helpless in the face of overarching peril. Doctor Who was a grand adventure and would take you out of yourself.

> **"Behind the dry jokes and stoic manner lurked a creature of awesome power."**

The intersection between our mundane world and the Doctor's was also a key imaginative trope. Stepping into something ordinary and finding yourself whisked across the galaxy... that's the same idea as the wardrobe in Narnia; and, as a kid, I was forever looking for something better than the drudgery of school.

Then there was the psychology of the Doctor. He was sexless but his companions were not. As a girl I was always trying to fathom him. But there was a strong sense that behind the dry jokes and stoic manner there lurked a creature of awesome power. Another childhood fantasy — that we can be much more than we seem.

For me, Doctor Who was strictly Baker (Tom). Every other Doctor before or since has been so lame by comparison they barely register on the scale. Perhaps the sole exception here is Christopher Eccleston. If he had succeeded Baker I would have stayed watching for longer. In my humble opinion, the show does not work if there are too many jokes and not enough terror.

The Doctor is an ancient creature, mighty in the extreme. When actors forget that in favour of hokiness and a quick laugh the whole premise of the thing is ruined. Every good fairy story has darkness at its heart.

Michael Legge

Comedian
Had his Edinburgh show posters designed to look like a Target Doctor Who novelisation cover

The thing that you have to know about me first of all is that I'm totally cool and popular. I'm pretty amazing and often get invited to parties and events. I went to a shindig once. That's just the type of rock-hard, sexually attractive man I am. Men want to be me and women want to be me too.

Well, I was at a party in North London when I was 25 years old and I was talking to some supermodels — or gothy looking drama students, I can't remember which — about the works of Woody Allen. I'm also very clever, did I mention that? So there I was talking about Zelig and Manhattan and watching red-hot ladies yawn with interest when a man approached and said, "Hello, Michael. I'm Brian."

Turns out Brian and I were in the same class when we were nine. "This must be lovely for him," I thought. "He's been spending the last 16 years or so wondering what happened to the awesome Michael Legge, the nuclear-powered love-tiger from primary school." Was I a stuntman now? An astronaut? A professor of women? He must have so many questions.

"So, Michael," said Brian to me, in front of all the equivalent of babes, "You still into Doctor Who?"

What? Why did he say that? I've never been into Doctor Who. That's for geeks. I loved sensitive films like Gregory's Girl and Dazed and Confused. I like The Smiths and Dead Can Dance. What a stupid thing for Brian to say. He was wrong, plus all the girls were looking embarrassed. "But you used to talk about Doctor Who all the time. You cried when Jon Pertwee left".

It was like Brian had opened up my own personal Chameleon Arch. How had I forgotten Doctor Who? I know Star Wars came along and stole my affections but, my God, I loved Who for years.

> **"It was like he opened up my own personal Chameleon Arch."**

How could I forget? In one second flat at a party in North London I remembered everything. I remembered the sonic screwdriver and Sarah Jane Smith and Venusian karate. In my head I could clearly see the Sea Devils rising up out of the water, the single most terrifying thing I saw as a child that genuinely made me hide behind the sofa. I remembered collecting Doctor Who pop-out cardboard figures given away free with a popular cereal and could actually taste Weetabix in my mouth.

And that is my favourite memory of Doctor Who, the fact that I forgot it. I spent the rest of the evening talking about *The Green Death* while the ladies I tried to woo walked away.

It's been the same ever since.

Philip Plait

American astronomer, author of Death from the Skies
Featured on Sylvester McCoy's Three Doctors quiz team at DragonCon 2011

First off, let's get this clear: I love Doctor Who. Don't believe me? One of the conditions I made for Discover Magazine to host my blog is that I would be able to write about the Doctor any time I wanted to.

Yeah, it's *that* important. Are we straight here? Good.

It was during the Tom Baker years (shown on public TV in the States) when I became truly Whoed. I never missed it. I had a floppy hat. My mom considered knitting me a scarf (an idea wisely dropped when she discovered its length).

In college we gathered on Sundays to watch the Peter Davison episodes... Then suddenly, sadly, TV stations weren't showing it anymore. I read all the books, all the comics. But there wasn't much I could do. My interest waned.

Until 2005. Then I found the rumours were true, and shortly thereafter there was Christopher Eccleston on my screen and, while he dressed more normally than I expected, he was clearly a Time Lord. I knew the Doctor had come back home.

My daughter was nine at the time. After I'd watched a few of the new episodes, I figured she might be interested in the show — she'd watched Firefly with me, and a few other "adult" dramas. So I plonked her down, explained to her who the Doctor was, who Rose was ("Don't tell Mom I think she's a hottie!"), and off we went.

"To my delight and joy, my daughter became as hooked as me."

To my delight and joy, she became as hooked as me. We watched together; as he beat the Slitheen; as he fought the Daleks; as he regenerated; and we waited out the new Doctor with trepidation, only to fall in love with him as well.

Then, during *Tooth and Claw*, a marvellous thing happened. My wife — not a fan — walked by, and saw the werewolf. "I love werewolves!" she said, and sat with us. And then sat again for *School Reunion*, and *The Girl in the Fireplace*... and then, miraculously, my whole family was watching the good Doctor saving the day; sacrificing himself, enjoying his companions, but yet, somehow, always being lonely.

But that's where fiction ends and reality begins, because I'm not lonely. I get to share one of my deepest and most cherished experiences with the people I love. In fact, that's a running theme on Doctor Who, and one I hope everyone gets to feel.

Oh, and about that Discover Magazine demand? When I relayed it to the publisher's CEO, he didn't bat an eyelash. "I love Cybermen! Bring on the Sontarans!" he said to me.

I knew then I was home, too.

Peter Howell

Musician, former BBC Radiophonic Workshop composer
*Spent six weeks in the summer of 1980 creating a new
arrangement of the Doctor Who theme*

Final mixes for Doctor Who were always very tight for time.
This was the case with any series — for the first few programmes
in the run, all went well, but gradually things got behind, which
meant that there was an increasing amount of things to do when
we reached the final mix. Not the best time to play a practical joke.
However that is exactly what happened.

While working on the music for *Meglos*, the post-production team
and I tried to trick the producer, John Nathan-Turner — something
which spectacularly backfired.

There was a scene in which one of the characters — I think it
was Lexa — was grabbed by the Doctor and escorted out of the
room housing the Dodecahedron.
The way that he grabbed her, both of
them extending their arms forwards,
reminded me of the sort of thing you
see in a tango. So, instead of the usual
music, I substituted a piece of ballroom
(I think it was a piece called Hernando's
Hideaway). It worked a treat. Doctor Who and Lexa did a turn
worthy of Strictly Come Dancing.

> "Instead of the usual
> music, I substituted a
> piece of ballroom."

Of course, I had composed a proper incidental piece of music
which was waiting secretly on another track; when John noticed
the gaffe, as we all expected, we would have a good laugh,
and simply replace the joke piece with the real one. You must
remember that in those days, before computerised mixing, the
final mix needed to be assembled from beginning to end, so the
replacement would need to be done as soon as it was heard.

The trouble was: John never noticed anything was wrong.

We all looked at one another not knowing what to do, as the
programme played on. In fact, no one said anything for the whole
episode. We were left with a finished soundtrack which contained

a piece of music we had no rights to, and the uncomfortable job of telling the show's producer he hadn't been paying attention.

We reluctantly came clean and, in fact, he took it very well but clearly thought the whole thing rather a waste of time. After all, we would now have to play the whole programme out again with the correct music. Funny when you look back on it but it did rather put me off playing tricks... although whenever I see that scene, I still hear the joke music in my mind.

Huw Turbervill
Cricket writer for the Daily Telegraph
Once recognised a cabbie as having played a crewman in Nightmare of Eden

I'm a rare breed: a cricket fan and Doctor Who devotee.

Sport and Who don't tend to mix. Who fans get upset when their show is delayed by an hour (or a week) because of an FA Cup semi-final, for instance, whereas sporty types are more worried about handballs than Handbots. But, for (the then-aged-nine) me, the enthusiasm Peter Davison's Fifth Doctor showed for cricket was thrilling. This Doctor kept his own pavilion in the TARDIS.

However, apart from a (scientifically dubious) trick with a cricket ball in *Four to Doomsday*, and a reference to Sharez Jek being "more a tennis player than a cricketer" — John McEnroe? — we don't actually see much cricket.

With one exception.

Black Orchid has the Doctor playing in an English country house match in 1925. He goes in at 56 (runs) for nine (wickets) — i.e. deep doo-doo — and helps rescue his side with a century. There are lots of "slogs" — I'm guessing Davison was a handy-ish club player — and it's clear director Ron Jones just didn't know his (Graham) Onions. The umpire signals a wide after the Doctor hits a four, for one thing. But there are nice touches.

"The Master was Jack Hobbs, of course."

The Doctor's bowling is better, even though he exaggerates when he tells his captain he is "fast" — he's "medium" at best — and then bundles the opposition out.

"A superb innings, worthy of the Master," the Doctor is told. He fears his arch foe is in town, but is relieved when the admirer says he is referring to WG Grace.

The Master was Jack Hobbs, of course, but I'll let it pass.

I'm hoping someone, someday will allow me to write another Doctor Who cricket tale. In my story, the Earth is under threat from a cricket-loving megalomaniac who has constructed an XI out of robots. Using the time scoop, the Doctor collects a side to vanquish them: Gooch, Tendulkar, Bradman, Lara, Richards, Sobers, Botham, Hadlee, Warne, Lillee. I'm padded up and ready to type!

Paul Cornell

Novelist, comic book and TV writer
Received a letter of praise for his Doctor Who stories from Kate Bush

I'm in the woods at the back of my school, and I'm among a bunch of girls and boys aged eight and nine and we've decided we're going to "have a fight".

We start dividing into two groups and, gradually, everyone steps away from this one girl who was never particularly unpopular until then (or maybe I just never noticed), and it's just me left standing with her.

> **"I wondered, at that moment, what Doctor Who would do."**

My friend Thomas calls me to come and join their side. But that would leave just her to be attacked by that whole bunch of kids, me included.

I don't remember her name, but I do remember that I wondered, at that moment, what Doctor Who would do.

The Doctor in my head was Jon Pertwee — as experienced only through the novelisations of Terrance Dicks — often spoken to me in the voice of my dad, though I was reading myself by then. I decided that he'd rather be the one being attacked than be part of a gang attacking one person. So I stayed put...

The other lot have at us. Much grabbing of sleeves, spinning around and being thrown over later, the others run off to do something else, and I'm left sitting with the little girl. Who tells me I didn't fight hard enough and that I smell.

But I'm pretty happy with myself. And I continue to be.

Andy Nyman

Actor, writer, director and magician
Was given the War of the Daleks board game as a present for his 44th birthday

My most frightening Doctor Who experience happened when I was about six years old.

I'll come clean, I'm not a die hard Who fan. I was of the Pertwee generation and to me he will always be the Doctor. I never really progressed from him. I suppose it's like your first love, to stray from them always feels so very difficult.

"Fear coursed through me and I grabbed my sister's hand."

Like so many others I have genuine and vivid memories of hiding behind the sofa when the dreaded "Exterminate!" razored its way out of an oncoming Dalek. But the creatures that really filled me with dread were the Cybermen. I think it was the combo of the unstoppable robot with it's semi-human guise that made it so disturbing to me.

But back to my moment of true terror. We were having a family weekend in Blackpool when we stumbled upon the Doctor Who exhibition. It was a different world then and the chance of being able to actually see the Doctor's props, let alone the TARDIS, seemed too much. It didn't occur to my six-year-old brain, as my slightly elder sister and I paid for our entry tickets, that the exhibition might also display some of the monsters.

We entered the first dark corridor, walking side by side, families of strangers either side of us. As we turned the first corner, there in all it's tin-foil terrifying glory, was a full-size Cyberman. A jolt of fear coursed through me and I grabbed my sister's hand and didn't let go until we exited that dark and scary corridor.

As we entered the light, the real terror struck me. The hand I was holding wasn't my sister's at all, but that of a stranger! I looked up at the dad of someone else's family, my sister about 12 paces behind us. True horror!

Toby Hadoke

Comedian
Created the one-man stand-up show, Moths Ate My Doctor Who Scarf

You always remember your first time. Occasionally, people I knew had met someone from Doctor Who. A friend's mum knew a bloke who apparently played "a cabbage monster" once, and my brother did a child-acting part with a man from *The Green Death* and someone called Edward Woodward (who'd never been in Doctor Who so wasn't worth meeting). Once I'd learned the names of the actors from all the old episodes, I made sure I went to the theatre to see them in action. As a kid I was introduced to Shakespeare because his words were being spoken by Varga, the Ice Warrior (alongside, less interestingly, some McCoy bloke from Tiswas), Dr Fendleman and Madame Lamia.

> **"The Sixth Doctor was coming to a theatre near me!"**

Then it happened. A Doctor — the Sixth Doctor — was coming to a theatre near me! I needed to be driven, and my grown up friend Derek had a car and, fortunately, few of my social inadequacies. He knew about meeting actors at stage doors, though we ultimately (and mistakenly) entered through the tradesman's entrance and found ourselves on the stage. Derek bravely bluffed our way past a friendly stage manager to the door of Dressing Room 1, knocked upon it, and a familiar voice greeted us warmly and invited us in. I remember little else apart from (and this time Derek made me do the talking, for my own good) asking for an interview for a fanzine I was planning.

The following Wednesday, I returned and interviewed a patient, warm, charming, and encouraging Doctor Who, who continued answering until my questions were exhausted (I can still hear the five minute call a fully civvied actor ignored to discuss *Terror of the Vervoids*) and bade me a cheery farewell. I wrote to thank him (I was well brought up) and he sent a courteous reply (he was too, then).

He was the first actor from the series I met properly. And the best. I've since met loads, worked with many, befriended others. None have quite matched how perfect Colin Baker made that encounter. And years after he'd forgotten our meeting, he nonetheless proved he'd not lost it by agreeing to do a cameo in my radio play.

I was now working with the Doctor in a professional capacity! Lovely, flattering, and even, yes, exciting — but work nonetheless. Giddyness had to give way to professionalism. A sign, perhaps, that you lose that childhood glee, that potential for the heart to skip a beat and to be tongue tied, awkward and thrilled like only a kid can. An innocence lost, and one that would never return to a cynical old grown-up who knows that actors are only people like everyone else.

Sad, you think, that you'll never recapture that feeling.

And then, without notice, you get a phone call from David Tennant while he's filming an episode of Doctor Who...

But that's another story...

Paul Putner

Actor and comedian
Appeared in BBC2's Doctor Who Night sketches alongside Mark Gatiss and David Walliams

1975. Nine years old. I was so engrossed in playing an imaginary game of Frankenstein meets the Hulk down the local rec that I had completely forgotten to come home for tea-time. Worse than the impending bollocking I would soon receive was the heart-plunging realisation that I'd also missed the last episode of *Genesis of the Daleks*. What an idiot! Missing your favourite

TV programme back then was an inconceivable horror, as you genuinely believed you would never, ever, ever, ever see it again.

I did not.

1979. 13 years old. I purchased the vinyl audio version of *Genesis of the Daleks* for £2.49 from WHSmiths. I discovered, after repeated listenings, it allowed me to perfect a quite passable impression of wibbly-voiced Davros, the evil git-in-a-bucket creator of the Daleks.

The trick is to gargle air, making the back of your tongue vibrate on the base of your upper soft palate. Then simply attempt to articulate typical Davros phrases such as, "You have the audacity to interrupt me?" or "You have the audacity to exterminate me, you ungrateful treacherous tin bastards?"

Next, you have to find the right attitude. Think of a piles-afflicted Kenneth Williams getting a bit waspish on Parkinson, then apply the razor menace of my old maths teacher, Mr Reed and finally, Adolf Hitler.

Start quiet, build slowly and crescendo with maniacal barking proclamations of universal genocide until eventually you're physically manhandled out the double maths lesson. Got all that? You can now do Davros. Have a jelly baby.

"Finally I was able to show off my nerdy party piece."

1998. 32 years old. I join the cast of Lee and Herring's anarchic BBC2 comedy show, This Morning with Richard Not Judy. I was The Curious Orange, a nervous citrus fruit who, over the course of the series, gradually develops megalomania and mutates into a vengeful, screeching, despot, orangey, Davros-hybrid-thingy rip-off. Finally I was able to show off my nerdy party piece, live, to the 1.2 million hungover students of Britain.

And one retired police officer who wrote in to complain about the show, remarking that I was "idiotic". He had a point. I had missed the last episode of *Genesis of the Daleks*.

Richard Wiseman

Professor, psychologist, author and magician,
Chatted to Jon Pertwee in the green room of This Morning in 1996

Strangely, my two most cherished memories of Doctor Who do not involve watching the television series. Instead, they both involve breakfast cereal.

When I was about 10 I saw the film Daleks – Invasion Earth: 2150 AD, with Peter Cushing playing the role of Dr Who. I thought it was great, and was especially delighted to discover that Sugar Puffs had sponsored the film, and that several scenes contained carefully placed advertisements for the cereal. I have always wanted to know whether the Daleks had been informed that their film was going to involve product placement and, assuming this was the case, how they felt about the ethics of this early example of overt marketing.

"I have always wanted to know how the Daleks felt about product placement."

My second memory involves that Weetabix promotion. I can vividly remember the excitement of pushing my brother out of the way, ripping open the packet (being careful not to tear the scene on the back) and seeing which cardboard Doctor Who figures fate had thrown my way. This sense of anticipation was matched only by the disappointment of discovering that I was now the proud owner of yet another bloody Silurian. Unlike the robust and dumpy Yetis, the Silurians had thin bodies and big heads, which meant that they had the habit of toppling over during crucial moments in my pretend adventures. Nevertheless, I spent many a delighted hour acting out my own Doctor Who stories using the figures and scenes. If I remember correctly, my most interesting production involved both the Doctor and Davros drinking a love potion and falling for one another. The mind boggles.

So, there we have it. For me, Doctor Who is all about Sugar Puffs, Weetabix, top heavy Silurians, and Davros exploring his more feminine side.

Tracy-Ann Oberman

Actress and writer
Used to receive Alex Kingston's fan mail

Was I scared?

When Doctor Who returned, yes, I was scared. Scared, along with everyone else, that my sacred childhood Saturday-night-compulsory-viewing memories were going to be trashed.

Memories of spaceships, and giant rats, and dinosaurs menacing cargo ships on the Indian Ocean. And the Daleks, and the Brigadier, and every invasion of Earth; I really bought into it. The whole concept of this lone Time Lord fighting evil was scary and the sense that anything might, could or would happen was quite enough to keep me in a state of childish agitation for a whole episode. And when a spider jumped on kindly uncle-type Jon Pertwee's back, turned blue and transformed him into a large hairy man with an all-consuming scarf… well, that bit was the scariest.

> **"I was secretly pleased to be one of the first to find out about Torchwood."**

So I can't say I'd ever dreamt I'd end up in the programme. Not until I saw the first Christopher Eccleston episode. I used to pretend I was Romana, all ethereal and cool — I think I once saw Lalla Ward play Ophelia to Derek Jacobi's Hamlet and I decided, quite rightly, that she was a great actress. But seeing Doctor Who come back, brighter and shinier and basically amazing, meant I was incredibly excited when I knew I was going to be part of it, especially being with David Tennant during his first series. (As a fan, I was also secretly pleased to be one of the first to find out how the Torchwood enigma unravelled.)

Our first day of filming together was in a discarded nuclear bunker — a ginormous set all beautifully lit in gold and black — and David and I were freezing. The buzz on set was palpable and I thought, "Wow! This is the best job ever". Yvonne Hartman was a great character; not quite evil, just misguided. Russell T Davies said to me at the time that I should think of her as the woman who went in to the BBC as the filing clerk and, through sheer determination,

people skills, charm and ruthlessness, ended up running the network. I love that her Top Trump card has a low fear factor but very high intelligence. My nephews have pointed this out to me over the years.

Yvonne had her redemption in the end. She overrode her Cyber-programming to save the world, "For Queen and country" — it was my favourite line. I've signed that many, many times on fan cards. I only wish I'd kept some of my own childhood Doctor Who memorabilia. It all got thrown away by my mum in various house moves. All those sacred Saturday-night-compulsive-playing toys — trashed. Sob!

Sam Watts

Musician, composer
Orchestrated the score to The Shakespeare Code *in Murray Gold's kitchen*

It was a sunny day in June 2009, and I'd been invited onto the set of The Sarah Jane Adventures for the filming of the third series' story, *The Wedding of Sarah Jane Smith*. I remember watching Lis Sladen and Nigel Havers filming scenes together. It was wonderful witnessing two talented, seasoned actors enjoying the material they had to play with, both taking notes from director, Joss Agnew, hitting their marks and nailing each of the few takes needed to film the scene.

> **"Lis jumped up, full of energy, ready and raring to go."**

Joss called "cut" and we all had the chance to chat a little. Nigel was a lovely, warm gentleman in the traditional sense of the word. He and Lis were both so down-to-earth and friendly. They giggled conspiratorially and got on like a house on fire. That day filming is one of my favourite memories of working on the show.

Later in the day, in a break from recording, after Lis had been running up and down stairs repeatedly, she sat down next to me on a sofa. She said how grateful she was for the chance to play Sarah Jane again and how lucky she felt that Russell T Davies and Julie Gardner had asked her back onto Doctor Who. She said something like, "Who'd have thought a series would have come out of it?". Then she leant over and told me, slightly conspiratorially, that she was finding the show's schedule tiring. You would never have known it, as she sat there in an ivory wedding dress looking stunning. Then the call came to restart and Lis jumped up, full of energy like an 18-year-old, ready and raring to go. Filming began and she was soon running up and down stairs again.

She was so generous and kind to those around her, something I was reminded of when I saw her after the Music from Outer Space concert she and her husband presented in Liverpool later the same year. The Royal Liverpool Philharmonic Orchestra played the Sarah Jane theme and a medley of my music from the show. She welcomed my partner and me into the dressing room after the concert with big hugs and smiles. My lasting memory of Lis, not that I knew her well, is of this enthusiastic, big-hearted, warm woman who enjoyed every minute of her time on the show.

Peter Anghelides
Writer
Visited the studio recording of Timelash *in 1984*

"'I can remember my 24th birthday party like it was yesterday,' said Shar Mozarno. 'But I can't recall what I had for lunch today.'"

I wrote those opening words in my 1999 Doctor Who novel, Frontier Worlds, intended as a funny comment about short-term memory. In our Wikipedia world, we joke about "memory like a sieve" or "having a senior moment". But in the character of Mozarno, I also had in mind someone else.

"As always, the Doctor makes things better."

I remember being moved to tears by the story of conductor Clive Wearing, related by Jonathan Miller in the Equinox documentary, Prisoner of Consciousness, on Channel 4 in 1986. At the age of 46, Clive contracted *herpes simplex encephalitis*. Usually the virus only causes cold sores, but in this case it affected his brain so badly that he became unable to form new memories — anterograde amnesia, which is also one of the symptoms of Alzheimer's.

For Clive, every conscious moment is like waking up for the first time. He can makes notes on paper, minute-by-minute, one after the other, and have no recollection of having written the preceding annotation. When his wife enters the room after only the briefest absence, he welcomes her as though she has been away for months.

So that's how I concluded my novel: Mozarno greeting his wife as she returns. The rest of the book is chases and explosions, villains and aliens, jokes and impressions. As always, the Doctor makes things better. But not for Mozarno, whose life cannot change. For him, as for Clive, what's now is now.

Deborah Wearing writes movingly about her life with Clive over two decades in her book, Forever Today: A True Story of Lost Memory and Never-Ending Love. I couldn't remember the title just now. So I looked it up online, obviously. I've got a memory like a sieve.

Jon Culshaw

Impressionist and comedian
Developed a phobia of Christmas puddings after seeing the Sontaran's head revealed in The Time Warrior

I could see Doctor Who everywhere when I was a lad. My dad once let me take a corner of his shed, paint it white and stick some paper plates to the wall so it was like a TARDIS. When I played, I would slowly open the door, wander out and imagine that I'd just landed on an alien world.

In my home town, just along the lane, there was a mushroom farm which was a big, industrial sort of place. It looked like a location straight out of *Inferno*. Long corridors to run down; lots of places to explore and pretend that you were the Doctor saving the solar system. I'd wear my long, navy blue duffel coat, just like the one Jon Pertwee would wear. He had a great sharpness to him, Pertwee, and a brilliant sort of elegance.

I once bought a pair of those white trainer boots that Peter Davison sported as part of his costume. I wore them to school one day with the regulation black uniform. My God, I got the mickey taken out of me that morning. Luckily, because I lived nearby, I'd go home for lunch so I changed my shoes later that day and put my school ones back on.

My sport at school was running. Part of the cross-country course ran through countryside, among farmland and hills, where the view looked rather like that scene in *The Five Doctors* with the Raston Warrior Robot. You could just imagine about 15 Cybermen marching up and being massacred. I used to say to my friends, "Stop now! Freeze. If you move, we're dead!"

"Those anniversary stories were my favourites."

Those anniversary stories were my favourites. I loved *The Three Doctors*. It was a special moment, to watch these towering, profound, enigmatic characters joining forces, when I was so used to seeing them acting alone for long chapters of the show. It signified a real emergency — when things like really, like, kick off, like, then you gotta get your own selves together to fix it all up, y' know worra mean — and fired the imagination. As if, should there be a big emergency in Noel Edmonds' universe, he'd have to go back in time and pluck out his Top of the Pops, Swap Shop and House Party selves to come and rescue a particularly sticky episode of Deal or No Deal.

But most vividly, my first memory of Doctor Who was the title sequence, when Jon Pertwee's face would appear and then sort of melt and get washed away. I remember my reaction was one of concern: "Oh, I hope it doesn't hurt him when his face gets all mushed up like that."

Janet Fielding
Actress, played the Doctor's companion Tegan
Snuck out of the studio recording of Kinda *to watch Ry Cooder perform on The Old Grey Whistle Test*

John Nathan-Turner, God love him, was the most wonderful producer that Strictly Come Dancing never had. He could have run the civil service. He could have run MI6. But John was a showman, and he did rather fancy himself as someone who knew a little about costumes. This, from a man who wore Hawaiian shirts.

For *Snakedance*, he decided to put me in a boob tube. A *boob tube*! I mean to say, the thing was bloody *hideous*.

One afternoon, after lunch, I was due to record some of the "possession by snake" scenes. When I'd done *Kinda*, they'd treated the voice but I thought it still sounded like me — it still had the cadence of me in it — so I was trying to make myself sound not like me, to alter my breathing rhythms so that I sounded different.

"In the middle of Television Centre, the booblings were out!"

So I was walking through the corridors of Television Centre, thinking about all this, and I had in my hands — I remember this vividly — a pocket book and a handbag. I was just about to go off to my dressing room when Peter Davison popped up and said, "Put down your bag, Janet" and so I did.

Then he said, "Put your hands up," and I thought — *what*? But I did it. I don't know why I did it except that I wasn't really thinking about what he was asking. I was on automatic pilot.

Out I popped.

In the middle of the doughnut at Television Centre, the booblings were out! The cameramen were coming through one set of doors and the actors were coming through another set of doors. At the time I was acutely embarrassed. It was really evil. Peter ran off into the make-up room. He was laughing so hard they couldn't get the make-up on him!

I never did get my revenge but, hey, we've all stayed friends and we see each other on a regular basis because we do the Doctor Who DVDs, which is really lovely. In fact, Peter and I are both members of Soho House. We were in there one night and we got talking to Jonny Lee Miller, a huge film star, of course. Peter, as he is wont to do, told him the boob tube story and, somehow, the conversation got around to *Kinda*. "Oh, yes, I know *Kinda*," said Johnny. "As a seven-year-old, I was an extra in it!"

John Nathan-Turner: he was no good with costumes but, boy could he spot talent.

Patrick Chapman

Poet and screenwriter
Wrote Fear of the Daleks, a Doctor Who audio book read by Wendy Padbury

How would you feel about being turned into plant food?

When I was eight, it was the scariest thing in the world. As someone who was born in the middle of the Troughton era — though I am aware other people refer to it as the late 1960s — I found myself coming of "Doctor Who age" in the mid-1970s. Tom Baker was my Doctor.

And the moment that first really scared the bejesus out of me? It's one of the cliffhangers of *The Seeds of Doom*. No, it's not when a Bonkers Millionaire™ called Harrison Chase kills a soldier by putting him into a compost machine to feed the Krynoids. That's not the scary bit. The scary bit is when, later, he tries to do the same to Sarah Jane Smith.

It's skillful writing to show the audience the horror of the machine, by offing a "redshirt" (to borrow a term from another show), then to threaten Sarah with the same fate. Chekhov's composter, if you will. That moment of bone-crushing terror was so effective not because of what was going on at the Krynoid end of the machine, but what was happening at the human end. There was a real person doing awful things to the Doctor's companion. The imagined horror of it was very powerful to a child. It really stayed with me and fired my imagination as well as my childish fear.

"The imagined horror was very powerful to a child."

Although I didn't know it at the time, I was living through the so-called "gothic horror" years of producer Philip Hinchcliffe and script editor Robert Holmes and this, I think, is my favourite era of the old show. There would be other scares after that — including, believe it or not, the weird eyebrows in *The Invisible Enemy* — but the human monster in *The Seeds of Doom* was far scarier.

I guess the human monsters always are.

Iain Lee

Broadcaster and comedian
As a three-year-old, was given two sugar cubes by Tom Baker in the BBC Club bar

For a long long time, in the 1970s and 1980s, my dad worked as a props buyer at the BBC. He's long since left there now so I think I can say, quite safely, that he would often steal stuff. I remember he stole me what he claimed was a bike from Grange Hill. So I used to ride around our lovely little council estate on the Raleigh Grifter ostensibly owned by Pogo Patterson.

"Right inside our garage was a genuine Dalek!"

Round the corner we had some of those lock-up garages. One day, my dad came in and said, "I've got something a little special to show you." I was probably about six years old. He told me, "You've got to come to the garage. I've got something exciting. It's a little bit scary but don't worry, because I'm going to be there. Let's just go and have a look to see what it is."

My sister and I thought, "What the hell is this? This is all a little bit weird!" but round we traipsed. It must have been about mid-afternoon. Dad unlocked the garage, lifted up the door and… right inside, there was a genuine Dalek!

Just awesome.

I didn't quite wet myself, but I was scared for a little bit. Obviously, it didn't move about on its own — so my dad had to go in, push it out and open it up. I think my sister got in there first but we took it in turns to be wheeled around. I was pulling on the levers and the plunger, shouting "Exterminate!" at the top of my voice. There were a lot of jealous kids so we had to keep it a bit quiet! Just because it was borrowed without permission (although I think we may have been taking it to a school fete to raise money, so that might have been the reason). If the people on the Britwell Estate in Slough had known there was a Dalek just sitting in a garage, then that lock-up would have been busted open.

Unfortunately, he had to take it back eventually. I've still got a wonderful picture somewhere, of me and my sister just standing in front of the Dalek, with me trying to look really tough and hard, but actually looking like a nob. The stuff my dad came home with was shocking! But, hey, man, it was the 1970s! The BBC was a lot slacker in those days.

Wincey Willis

Broadcaster, former TV-am weather girl
Has been namechecked in a number of scripts by Russell T Davies

My oldest friend died before her granddaughter, Kate, was born and I was lucky enough to be able to act as a surrogate granny to her. Her mummy married a man who already had a son, Tom Hargreaves, who is quite a bit older than Kate and he is an absolute Doctor Who fanatic, with a capital "f" — to the point where he could go on Mastermind and win, I'm sure.

Now, I'm old enough to remember all the Doctors, so I vividly recall the black and white ones with William Hartnell. Despite what it says on Wikipedia, which claims I have about 10 different ages, I was a small child when I watched those and was immediately captivated by them.

> **"He could go on Mastermind and win, I'm sure."**

Looking back, I remember people would say, "Oh it's so frightening," and hide behind the sofa. Well, I never felt frightened at all. I just enjoyed it. I got terribly excited by it all — even the sight of the Daleks; and especially that quarry that was on every planet they visited.

There was, however, a whole selection of Doctors that I didn't see at all because I was travelling. But I have since become a very great friend of Colin Baker's. We were both vice presidents of the trust at Tiggywinkles Wildlife Hospital and we worked together on that for quite some time. We've remained friends ever since.

So, because I knew Tom, I secretly got a big signed photograph from Colin and took it down to his house in Truro and said,

"Oh, I have something for you." He visibly shook as he saw it coming out of the envelope. He was in such a state, he couldn't believe it was real. He dashed upstairs and came back down with all of Colin's Doctor Who DVDs, so I had to then go off and get the sleeves signed too.

Tom wrote Colin a letter to say thank you and asked him a lot of questions. I taped all the answers, so now Tom has his own recorded interview, too. As a result, I can walk on water at the Hargreaves' house and I am *the* best surrogate step-granny ever! But do you know what my favourite thing is? After he'd got over the shaking and re-ordered his DVDs, he looked back at that signed photo and said, "I don't think Colin's pictured with the right TARDIS on there!"

Like I said, fanatic with a capital "f".

Tom Reynolds

Ambulance driver, author of Blood, Sweat and Tea
Wrote his first Doctor Who fan fiction when he was seven

I know you don't realise this, but I am very closely related to the Doctor.

Oh, you may think that I am your average ambulance-man, whizzing around on blue lights and sirens saving lives, but I am more like the Doctor than you would imagine.

First off, let's look at the vehicle. It's boxy, it's weird, it's full of strange machinery (including a machine that goes "Ping!") and I would swear blind that it is bigger on the inside. It also has a blue flashing light on top of it and it makes a strange noise when it's travelling.

It also breaks down a lot.

I wear an unusual set of clothes. Big and bulky and day-glo yellow. It has deep pockets full of equipment — stethoscopes, tools, drugs, huge scissors. It has even been known to carry the odd bag of jelly babies.

I travel with a companion. They are often a very attractive young woman whom I try to impress. I also don't have sex with them.

I once had a crewmate with a moustache (he wasn't a woman), but sadly he never said, "Chap with wings, there. Five rounds rapid." But I lived in hope that one day he would.

I often find myself mimicking the personality of the current Doctor (especially when dealing with children), normally by waving my arms around and grinning a lot. But, for some reason, I don't find myself copying the snotty crying of David Tennant.

"I am more like the Doctor than you would imagine."

For my adventures I arrive in my vehicle, dressed in my costume and take control when someone is having a really bad day. I bounce around, spout some jargon and leave with everyone generally a bit better off than they were before I arrived.

And no-one knows my name.

The Doctor and me? We're brothers.

Johnny Candon

Comedian
Giggled like a princess when Paul McGann shook his hand at a voice-over job

In 1978 I was five years old. My sister Anne was a year younger. On Saturdays, my older cousin John was forced to babysit us all day while my parents ran the local post office. His only stipulation was that he be allowed to watch Doctor Who undisturbed.

Bless him, that boy had patience! He indulged every whim, rescued us when we got stuck in trees and played every silly game we invented — once going so far as to be Scooby-Doo, with Anne as Daphne and me as The Man from Atlantis in a TV crossover event that sadly never made it out of our back garden.

John suffered all this and more just so that for 25 blissful minutes he could be transported away from demanding children and join the Doctor and Romana in their quest for the Key to Time.

Oh, we promised we'd sit quietly in the kitchen with colouring books — we possibly even believed we would — but as soon as the best theme tune in the world started, we'd run into the living room, turn the TV off and run away screeching with laughter. John used to chase us until he realised that was exactly the reason we were doing it and so he stopped.

"We'd run in, turn the TV off, and run away screeching."

We didn't, though. Every five minutes we'd run in, switch the TV off and disappear in hysterics. If you're reading this, John, I'm truly sorry. The thing is, my parents used to get in just as Doctor Who finished and you'd be off home. You see, Doctor Who was eating into the last hour we had with you and we resented it. We couldn't even watch it with you, it was so *terrifying*!

So, John, those annoying missed seconds were born out of love. You were big and funny and strong and brave enough to watch Doctor Who on your own. My hero then watching my hero now.

Therefore, I dedicate this to a gentle soul, who fired the imagination of children. Someone who was always patient and never cruel and who made Saturdays magical...

Sarah Greene

TV presenter, actress
Played Varne, a Cryon from the planet Telos, in
Attack of the Cybermen

In 1985, I got a call from my agent asking, "Would you like to do Doctor Who?" I fell about laughing because I hadn't been acting for a few years and this was such a legendary series on which to work. I'd only just finished doing Blue Peter.

It transpired that the person directing was someone I had worked with years before, on a soap called Together, and he'd obviously remembered me. They were also going through a phase of using people who were well known in other areas, so Faith Brown was in it and I think that they were planning to have either Sam Fox or Koo Stark too.

I thought it was very odd getting what you might call, in very shallow terms, a "face" to come on your show and then proceed to cover them up in layers and layers of plastic and Perspex, so that their face is completely obliterated. I can only assume that they used to bulk buy bubble wrap at the BBC — and on the planet Telos!

They spent an enormous amount of time and trouble taking whole head casts of us Cryon creatures. I was covered in plaster of Paris and had straws stuck up my nose and mouth. I've still got the cast — it's quite weird because it looks like a death mask. I think even one of my eyelashes is stuck in it. You can see how worried I looked because it captures the expression underneath. I defy anyone not to feel ill-at-ease when their head is covered completely.

"I can only assume that they used to bulk buy bubble wrap at the BBC."

You'd think that it would only get more comfortable after that. Unfortunately, the days it took to shoot the sequences I was involved in it were the hottest on record, and it was in the studios of Television Centre. No air conditioning. Our outfits were completely made of plastic, head to toe, so it was like being in a sauna.

Not only was it absolutely, stiflingly hot but it also happened to be the weekend when my then-boyfriend, now-husband, was away as part of the British Touring Car championship. They were racing in Germany that weekend and it was a fairly important race. By the time I got home, I was absolutely dehydrated, almost a bit dizzy and spinning. I picked up the phone to listen to the messages and found out he'd won! So, absolutely thrilled to bits, I went to the fridge and downed two cans of Stella.

He got home about midnight to find me lying on the floor, in the middle of our little sitting room, completely out for the count. I blame it on that bloody costume!

Charlie Brooker

Writer and broadcaster
Was disappointed when the Doctor didn't appear in the 2012 Olympic opening ceremony

Tom Baker was my Doctor, although I have a very clear memory of being scared witless at an early age by an episode from the Jon Pertwee era — the moment where the Auton shop window dummies come alive in *Spearhead from Space*. Since that was originally broadcast in 1970, and I wasn't alive until 1971, I must have been watching a repeat several years later. Maybe it travelled through time just to spook me. The dummies smash through a department store window and coldly gun down a policeman in the street — you see him lying there, stone dead — which I'm pretty sure wouldn't be allowed nowadays.

Anyway, I avidly watched the show during the Tom Baker years, and enjoyed it precisely because everything about it was so willfully weird and creepy. It had a kind of gleeful menace. Tom Baker was so downright strange you felt like he might pull mad, yet slightly threatening, faces at your back if you momentarily turned away the screen. Everyone spoke slightly too loudly, the spectre of death was ever-present, and the whole thing was backed with an eerie Radiophonic soundtrack which sounded like someone trying to tune a longwave radio in to the spirit realm. You could never relax while Doctor Who was on. You were on edge the whole time. It was brilliant.

> **"It was the first time I'd felt that thorough, down-to-the-bone chill."**

One thing that's slightly lacking from the new incarnation is the use of terrifying cliffhangers — those spine-tingling moments where the Doctor seems to be in mortal peril and the squealing end credit music comes wailing in. One in particular that sticks in my mind comes from a 1980 story called *The Leisure Hive*. (I had to look that up — I only saw it the once and scarcely dared watch it again.)

My understanding of what happens is this: the Doctor has entered a machine called the Recreation Generator, a sort of fantasy-to-

reality processer. As the Doctor enters the machine, an image of him appears on a screen outside. We're then told that whatever happens to the Doctor on the screen will actually physically happen to him *inside the machine* — like a voodoo doll. Then, suddenly, his arms and legs are pulled off! And his head comes off! And the camera crash zooms into Tom Baker's horrified face as Doctor Who screams — in agony. I repeat: *Doctor Who dies in screaming agony*! Right there on screen.

As his scream blended with the wailing end theme music, I turned cold, like I'd just witnessed a beheading. I was nine years old: it was the first time I'd felt that thorough, down-to-the-bone chill — the one you get from a thumping good fright scene, such as the climax of the original Japanese version of The Ring — and I've never forgotten it. Every time I sit down to watch a horror film I hope I'll get a similar shock. It rarely happens.

Nev Fountain

Writer
Shed a tear at Jamie and Zoe's farewell to the Doctor in The War Games

I'll tell you about the Doctor Who I didn't watch. *The Ribos Operation*, episode one. How the memory burns. It burns…

Travelling back from hols, Dad egging the car up to warp nine, alas too late to get home in time. We came in just as the closing credits "weeooowed". And wouldn't you just know it? It just happens to be the episode that explains the plot for the whole bloody season. Bloody Key to Time. Bloody overarching umbrella story arc bloody…

It's always the same with me and Doctor bloody Who. One year I left my teeny tiny home town for the summer holidays — at exactly the same week that Tom Baker arrives, scarf a-flying, to appear in my local WHSmiths. Total eclipses are more common than celebrities appearing in Stamford. The production team must have wired up my house and checked exactly when I was scheduled to go to Butlins so they could "put Tom in now", so to speak. Bloody Tom Baker. Bloody WHSmiths. I buy all my Target books from you and this is how you repay me? You give me no respect.

The first convention I pick to go to happens to be the one I can't get in to (and, no, I'm not telling you why), so all I get is a fleeting look at Peter Davison's back, K-9's voice in the distance and my dad picking a fight with Jon Pertwee.

"I chivalrously defended Peri's honour, of course."

The first episode I ever watched with a girlfriend (and, yes, I did have one) happened to be the rubbish last episode from *The Two Doctors*, which she merrily took the mickey out of from beginning to end. I chivalrously defended Peri's honour, of course, but when they did the "Do you serve humans here?" joke and the Sontarans started vomiting I crawled behind the sofa. Oh dear, I never thought I'd be back *there* again. However...

She's gone. Doctor Who's still here. Guess which one I loved the most.

Carol Decker

Recording artist, songwriter, singer with T'Pau
Felt very guilty for wanting to bed the Tenth Doctor

I find the idea of outer space, that relentless oblivion, really scary. When I was young I had a really over-active imagination. I was frightened of the dark for years and, even now, I hate deep, dark water. So I would never "play" at Doctor Who because I was worried that something would go wrong and we would be floating forever into nothingness.

I have to admit I remember William Hartnell. I recall the picture always being so grainy you could barely see the action. It was tea-time viewing so I'd be watching with my brother (we'd moved from Liverpool to Wellington in Shropshire so I think I was about seven and he was five). Dad would be pottering about doing DIY and ruining the house and mum would be making tea — as a treat, we could have it watching the telly in the front room.

Although my brother was younger than me, he was more excited than scared. I, on the other hand, always had a big cushion in my arms to lift up to my face in the event of there being too much tension. It was always the tension that got to me more than what I actually saw. The music, too, would help to build it — I learned the power that music had to effect emotions at a very early age. The theme tune in the 1960s was quite eerie and, perhaps because the show was in black and white, it was in some respects grittier and more sinister.

Patrick Troughton is probably "my" Doctor, as he made the most impact on me when I was at the right age to be pulled in to the show but, of course, I kept a weather eye on all the Doctors over the years.

> **"I learned the power that music had to effect emotions at an early age."**

It's almost a British tradition to watch Doctor Who — at least it is in my family. We are totally into the show now. My son Dylan, who is nine, collects all the toys and models. We've got a Dalek money box, all the character figures, the comics and even a TARDIS wardrobe. I've worked with David Tennant a couple of times (the highlight of my career was meeting him on Comic Relief, looking gorgeous in a kilt — I couldn't help wondering, "Is he a true Scotsman?") and had to shake a comedy fist at him. He's responsible for our house being filled with monsters and aliens. Thanks, Doctor. We are broke!

Mitch Benn
Musician, stand-up comedian
Wrote and sang an ode to Doctor Who girls on Radio 4

Adric was a wanker. Everybody knew that. Even those of us who were wankers ourselves. I was 12 and a Doctor Who fan. Most of my contemporaries were 12 or 13 and Doctor Who fans. So it's fair to say that most of my immediate circle of friends were fairly enthusiastic wankers in 1982, and even we knew a real wanker when we saw one. Look at him, with his "Davy Jones out of The Monkees" haircut and his pyjamas and his seeming inability to pronounce anything. Wanker.

> **"Right from the off, Earthshock was different."**

And then *Earthshock* happened.

Right from the off, *Earthshock* was different from any Doctor Who story we'd seen. Roger Limb's happy, farty Yamaha DX7 was replaced by Malcolm Clarke's icy musique concrète. Soldiers were being melted by some off-screen nasties. Even the (genuine) surprise Cybermen reveal, immensely cool though it was, couldn't dispel the feeling that This Wasn't Going To End Well. *Earthshock* had a grinding wrongness that one would later come to associate with really good Japanese horror movies, but I was 12 and they hadn't been invented so I had no contextual references at all.

It didn't end well.

Companions didn't die in Doctor Who. Not even the wankers. Yes, those of us immersed in fan literature had heard of Sara Kingdom and Katarina but the first had only been in one story and, as such, was a one-off supporting character and they died all the time. Real companions didn't die. For the last five minutes of episode four we were still wondering how the Doctor was going to save Adric, because Adric was a real companion and real companions don't die...

Boom.

As the credits rolled silently over the broken star of mathematical excellence, the universe became a chillier place, and a part of my childhood peace and innocence disappeared forever.

Amanda Lawrence

Actress
Played Doomfinger, an ancient Carrionite, in The Shakespeare Code

The Carrionites were witch-like beings from the dawn of the universe who used the power of words to do evil. Like politicians, really. Two other actresses — Linda Clarke and Christina Cole — played my "weird sisters" and all three of us had to wear full head prosthetics as part of the transformation. They looked incredibly real, though. I think we genuinely passed as 400-year-olds. My favourite memories of this time were the two night shoots we had to do at the Globe Theatre. Because we were filming on location and couldn't set up in the venue itself, we had to have all our costumes, wigs and make-up applied by a brilliant team based in a car park over by London Bridge. Once readied, assembled and groomed, we three suitably scary hags were required to climb into the back of a black car and be driven the short distance over to the Globe, from thence to start the crucial job of acting in front of the cameras.

> **"I offered a creeping, eerie smile and pointed at her with my very real talons."**

It was about 11pm on a Friday night. Pubs were emptying and the car moved at a crawl due to revellers and late-night London traffic. At one point, we slowed down near a bus stop. There were a few young people waiting for the next night bus to take them home or onward to another party. A woman was laughing and, as we stopped, she happened to look down at our car. I pushed my face to the window and tapped my long gnarled nails on the glass. As her eyes met mine, I offered a creeping, eerie smile and pointed at her with my very real talons...

Sadly, I cannot satisfactorily describe the extent to which her face completely dropped as she turned white with fear. I shot her a few more supernatural glances and then we drove off.

If she happens to ever read this — I'm so sorry to have done that... but it was very irresistible! Hopefully, she saw Doctor Who a few months later and made the connection.

Andrew Smith

Policeman, author
Became the youngest ever Doctor Who scriptwriter in 1980, when Full Circle *was commissioned*

There were TV shows that I followed avidly in my youth other than Doctor Who. But a visit to the Doctor Who Exhibition in October 1975 turned me into a pukka Doctor Who fan.

We were having a family break in Blackpool, a town we'd lived in briefly when I was young (my first memory in life is aged three, kicking a ball down into the scary basement of our house in Central Drive and being too afraid to go after it).

The exhibition building on the Golden Mile caught my eye from a distance. The colourful signage, bearing the Doctor Who diamond logo and promising the TARDIS and Daleks, beckoned my 12-year-old self like the world's biggest bag of sweets.

The entrance was itself a TARDIS. It was a thrill to walk through those blue doors and pass into the world of Doctor Who which, as it turned out, was to be found down a flight of steps. My first memory in life might have been a fear of descending into a Blackpool basement, but I couldn't wait to explore *this* one.

> "Brilliantly written, the Target books enriched my view of the world."

My strongest recollection is of one of the very first displays — the Giant Robot. There it was, the *real thing*, in all its sizeable glory. I was gobsmacked. The seeds of true fandom were planted in that moment. Germination was ensured as I continued round. Look there, the TARDIS control console, and there a Cyberman, a Dalek. Blimey, a Wirrn. Mum! Mum, that's a Sea Devil!

Then at the end of what, by today's standards, would be considered a disappointingly short sojourn through the displays, there was the shop. And what a shop this was. It had Target books, novelisations of Doctor Who stories. The range wasn't extensive, but the titles gripped me: Doctor Who and the Daleks; Doctor Who and the Cybermen; Doctor Who and the Abominable Snowmen. The list went on.

I'm not sure how many of the novels I bought that day, at least three. Brilliantly written, they enriched my view of the world of Doctor Who, which to that point I'd known only through TV.

I started writing my own "novels" from off-air recordings, learning about narrative, plotting and dialogue, until I decided I'd concentrate on my original material and start pestering Doctor Who script editors…

Luke Hyams

Writer, creator of Dubplate Drama
Bought a Peter Davison costume t-shirt especially for a trip to the Doctor Who Experience in 2011

It's 1995. Doctor Who has been off television for six years and is sorely missed in my household. I am at a BBC party, just a few feet away from BBC big-wig Alan Yentob, and closing in with one very important question on my mind...

Jump back to 1984. It's my fourth birthday and I have come downstairs shortly before dawn to find a plastic TARDIS tent has materialised in the middle of the living room. I am in awe. I step inside and sit down, basking in the blue plasticky magic for hours, not at all disappointed that it was actually rather poky inside.

Before He-Man, before Adam West, before Optimus Prime, Peter Davison was my first hero. The beige-clad knight who knew how to see off the Master and Davros, always remaining terribly polite while doing so. I loved every second of his years as the Doctor but was left quite confused when he left and the next time I saw him on TV he had his hand up a heifer's backside.

Fast forward nine years and I am at a car boot sale sifting through old back issues of Look-In and one-legged Barbies to find a much-cherished, third-hand VHS copy of *Genesis of the Daleks*. All of a sudden I realised why people who were born in the 1970s scoffed when I said that Peter Davison and Colin Baker were the best Doctors. Tom Baker's performance was a revelation. The hair, the smile, the

> **"Before He-Man, before Optimus Prime, Peter Davison was my first hero."**

jelly babies and the scarf. An appetite for new adventures from Gallifrey's favourite son was ignited — all the UK Gold repeats and fan-made films like Downtime and Shakedown could only do so much to satisfy my hunger.

So here I am in 1995. I'm confronting Alan Yentob and asking him when we'll get any more Doctor Who. I brace myself and am duly disappointed when he tells me that until the Beeb can stump up a million dollars per episode like Star Trek: The Next Generation, there is really no point in doing it.

Thank heavens it only took another 10 years for them to get their act together and give us back our Doctor Who. I am sure he will never ever leave us again.

Matthew Sweet

Writer, journalist and broadcaster
Presented a Radio 4 documentary about Delia Derbyshire, entitled Sculptress of Sound, in 2010

My earliest memories of Doctor Who are my earliest memories of anything: the Draconians, those Samurai lizards in shoulder pads, looming on a black-and-white set in the front room of a terrace in Hull — an image, which, for me, is irremediably associated with the taste of the glacé cherry on top of a Skelton's trifle. I worry about this sometimes, as I think many Doctor Who fans do — that the phrenological diagram of my brain would reveal that far too much space was devoted to the Fishmen of Kandalinga or the satellites of Grundel, and that this may be the reason I can't do long division or understand cricket scores. I can't remember being told the facts of life, but I do remember my dad sitting me down to tell me that Jon Pertwee was leaving Doctor Who.

"Kraal eyeballs goggling through a wall."

And then there's the question of moral influence. The man with the beard who did tricks with loaves and fishes never impressed me much. Tom Baker had more influence on the formation of my ethical character. He taught me that it is acceptable to heft a psychotic botanist into his own composter in order to prevent Krynoids devouring London, and that you should always gas a mad neu-rosurgeon if it means squishing his plot to resuscitate the brain of Morbius. 20 years later, I interviewed Tom Baker over a liquid lunch in Soho. This was his opening gambit: "I suppose you've just come down from Cambridge with a lower second and that you're *utterly commonplace*." And this from the man who was the reason why I felt compelled to stay at university long enough to get a D.Phil.

I now watch with my own children, who don't observe the distinction between old and new Doctor Who. They like Sylvester McCoy and anything with fanged monsters — *The Curse of Fenric*, *State of Decay*, *Vampires of Venice*, *Time and the Rani* — they can dip into any era of the programme as and when they please. I know how old I was when I saw Drashigs bursting from a swamp, Sea Devils burning through a submarine bulkhead, Kraal eyeballs goggling through a hole in the wall. If you were born in the 1960s or 1970s, you too may measure out your life in Doctor Who. And maybe for you too, *Frontier in Space* is a bright little image from the beginning of your life, and a kind of *memento mori*.

Una McCormack

Writer, lecturer in creative writing
Was catapulted off a bench by Terrance Dicks at a Doctor Who convention

One afternoon in the autumn of 1992, while I was still a student, I made my first post on the internet, to the university bulletin board devoted to Doctor Who. The substance of my email was my assessment of the story currently under consideration by the membership of the board, *The Android Invasion*. I wrote, "It's crap."

Some hours after this, I received my first flame.

My flamer (let's call him Flame Boy) courteously explained himself. For several months, he replied, he and others had been attempting to make the board less a seething stream of vitriol and more an arena for considered discussion. My contribution was not helping.

"Reader, I married him (sort of)."

Would I therefore care to offer some evidence to substantiate my claim of *The Android Invasion*'s crapness?

That seemed perfectly fair to me. So I offered some more opinions on the subject (I forget what they were now). "Thank you," said Flame Boy. "I broadly agree."

That was at the start of my final year at university. Time was rushing past, exams were looming, and the real world was waiting. But there were still a few golden months left, all of which I spent

136

with a gang of smart and funny young men who loved Doctor Who. And Blake's 7. And Robin of Sherwood. And… And…

We swapped videos. We grabbed time on a friend's PC to write and publish a fanzine. Some of us experienced unrequited love. Some of us experienced requited love.

Because, reader, I married him (sort of). Videos gave way to DVDs. Our show came back (twice). The internet didn't change very much. And Flame Boy and I continue to travel together through space and time, still holding broadly compatible opinions on *The Android Invasion*.

Lynda Bellingham

Actress, TV presenter
Played the Inquisitor in The Trial of a Time Lord

I got the Doctor Who job because Anita Graham, who is an actress, had her birthday party at my then ex-husband's restaurant in Muswell Hill, and John Nathan-Turner was a guest. He was sitting opposite me and he said, "Do you know what? I've got just the part for you. Do you think you could be stern and authoritative?" I said, "John, I'm an actress." To be honest, they don't often care, these producers!

"I did 13 weeks of Doctor Who entirely sitting down."

For my costume, they made me a huge white headdress with supports sticking out on either side to make it stand up. It was attached to the back of my neck so I couldn't actually move my head at all. They also gave me these long, false red nails so I could hardly do anything with my hands either. It was all very Joan Collins. What I remember most of all is that, if I ever wanted to go to the loo, I had to ask permission from the wardrobe department, who would then walk me to the toilet. They had to pull my tights down because I couldn't do anything with these false nails on and I couldn't look down because of my headdress. It was a bit like being a bride. I had to have help to do anything.

I also remember having a row with the BBC bureaucrats, who behaved in their inimitable, intractable way. Actors were never allowed to use the car park — everyone else could park their cars, but not the actors. They said to me, "Well, you can park it up the road and then you can move it closer to the theatre during your supper break."

I said, "You seriously want me to walk around White City in this lot, in the dark, and get my car? You'll be lucky if I come back alive!" I would have been in deep trouble had I stepped foot outside the building.

The bizarre thing was, of course, that I did 13 weeks entirely sitting down. At the start of the first episode, I walked into the courtroom for the trial and sat down — where I remained for the whole story. And in the 14th episode, I got up and walked out of the courtoom! Which is just as well — in that costume it was as much as I could do to stand up, really.

But I was very disappointed — I still *am* greatly disappointed, in fact — that I've never been asked back.

Terrance Dicks
Author, former script editor on Doctor Who
Based The Five Doctors *on Childe Roland to the Dark Tower Came by Robert Browning*

My time as Doctor Who's formal script editor came to an end in Jon Pertwee's fifth and final year when he decided, quite fairly if you ask me, that he'd been doing it long enough. Playing the Doctor is a trap for an actor. It's great while he's doing it — he's in regular work and he's a star — but, when he stops, everybody thinks of him as the Doctor. It's hard to get other work.

> "When I joined Doctor Who, I thought I'd take the job on for about three months."

He gave us plenty of notice. He came to me and Barry Letts and said, "I don't know how to tell you this. I really think that, after this season, I don't want to do another one."

And Barry said, "Well, I was thinking the same thing, actually". Barry had never wanted to be a producer. He was a director, that was his first love. He had a clause in his contract that allowed him to direct occasionally, so he directed Doctor Who whenever he got the chance. Barry became, and was, my best friend until his sad death. We were good friends for over 30 years. We worked together every day, and when we weren't working together, when there were gaps, we would have dinner together once a week to keep in touch.

So, with Jon and Barry going I thought I might was well go as well. I didn't want to feel like a spare part, an embarrassing sort of overhang, and I didn't think that I could stand any other producer — or probably that any other producer could stand me — so I went back to freelance writing,

Fortunately, before I left, Target books set up their children's line. A few Doctor Who novelisations had been published in hardback years before but hadn't done that well. Target bought them up, put them in bright covers, and they sold like hot cakes! So the editor came rushing to the production office and said, "I need some more Doctor Who books! Who's going to write them?"

I said, "I will!"

It wasn't a Machiavellian plot or anything, it just kind of fell into my hands. It was absolutely unjustified confidence, as I'd never written a book before. I did *Spearhead from Space* first, which they promptly rechristened The Auton Invasion. They used to change the titles a bit.

The thing about freelance is you need steady, regular work. I wrote up to around 70 novelisations, give or take. When I joined Doctor Who, I thought I'd only be doing it for about three months. Here I am over 40 years later still writing about it.

The nice thing is the number of elements from the show in our days that have reappeared since it came back to TV, partly I think because Russell T Davies was a great fan. They started off with our Autons. The Sontarans have done very well and the Silurians came up fairly recently, too.

So, you see, there's quite a bit of life left in these old monsters yet.

Frances Barber

Actress
Played Madame Kovarian in the 2011 series of Doctor Who

"By Silencio Lake on the Plain of Sighs an impossible astronaut will rise from the deep and strike the Time Lord dead."

I have to say, and I mean this, I think Matt Smith is probably the best casting of the Doctor ever, and for one particular reason. Matt Smith could be playing 19 or 119, and he would still convince me. He has one of those extraordinary, eccentric faces and sensibilities that come around very seldomly. You see people like him in paintings in art galleries. He looks like he was born in another century. I just think he's a brilliant actor and I can't think of anybody better to play Doctor Who, out of all of them.

Of course, when I was cast as his baddie, I was thrilled. And then when I had the costume fitting and the eye patch came up, I was beside myself. Plus, as far as I was concerned, I was just appearing in one episode, but then I kept popping up in others through little hatches, so it just kept getting better and better each time.

"It just kept getting better and better."

What I did find very difficult was learning the lines, because it's a science fiction world that I'm not au fait with. It's very particular, very specific and you have to be word perfect.

I asked Matt about it because of the volume of lines he has — masses of dialogue, which he delivers very, very fast, as is his forte — and he said he learned it like music. He would sit in his apartment in Cardiff and literally annotate the script like a musical score, as if he were singing it.

With Doctor Who scripts, there's no room for manoeuvre in terms of improvisation or being vague. Most of the time I didn't quite know what I was talking

about. (Like that prophecy, back up there. Of course, when I finally saw the episode, I was completely mesmerised and thought, "Oh my God, so that's what I was saying.")

And then they killed me.

Didn't they?

Alex Kingston said to me, "Oh darling, I've been killed four times, and I keep coming back." So that's what I'm hoping, that maybe Kovarian might make a return. Because there's nothing I'd like more.

James Moran
Screenwriter
Learned the word "capacious" from Target books

When it was warm enough — and usually even when it wasn't — I'd be playing outside with my mates on Doctor Who nights. It was safe though, because Darren's mum always shouted out, with minutes to spare — "Darren! Doctor Oo's on!" — and that was our Bat-Signal. We wouldn't even have to say goodbye to each other. Our unspoken code just meant we could immediately abandon our game, and run off home. Doctor Oo was too important for such time wasting pleasantries.

One of my strongest, earliest Doctor Who memories is of one such night. Racing home through the back garden, in the back door, and flinging myself in front of the TV, just in time for the opening sequence. My mother was always baffled as to why I'd watch "that sort of rubbish", or read the Target books, when there was "proper" telly to watch, and "proper" books to read. Tonight was the start of a new story, *City of Death*. The Doctor and Romana ran around Paris, quipping, bantering, clearly having a great time, while somewhere else in the city, mysterious goings-on were... going on.

"I didn't understand it half the time, but it was brilliant fun."

As usual, I didn't really understand it half the time, but it was brilliant fun. And you always knew that at the end of the first part of a new story there'd be the Cliffhanger, with the Scream leading into the End Credits. So when Scarlioni, for no apparent reason other than to give us a cool cliffhanger, pulls off his fake human face, revealing the spaghetti-ness of his real, alien face, I was thrilled. Who is he? What's he up to? Why's he got a spaghetti face? Blimey, he's got one big eye!

And that, ultimately, was why I watched the show and read the books. Because in "proper" TV shows, or "proper" books, the villain never pulls off his face to reveal a big, alien, spaghetti face. And that's why I loved it, and still do.

David Bradley

Journalist, editor of sci-fi magazine SFX
Stood next to Russell T Davies in the visa queue at the US embassy

I was just nine years old — too young, perhaps, to fall in love. But I couldn't take my eyes off the screen when Nyssa strode on in her mauve velvet dress.

> **"Black Orchid defines the moment when I became 'a fan'."**

It's often said that everybody remembers "their" first Doctor, but of course they remember their first companion too and the mere thought of Sarah Sutton would make me look forward to an episode all week. Although I vaguely remember Tom Baker and the companions of his final series, it was Davison's packed TARDIS (Tegan and Adric were also on board with Nyssa and the Fifth Doctor) that first became must-see television to this hopeless young romantic.

Imagine my delight — and some of my confused pre-adolescent dreams — when *Black Orchid* aired in 1982. Two of her! Almost too much for this young TARDIS fan to take as Nyssa and Ann Cranleigh met on screen. In retrospect, it's not actually one of the greatest serials but it does give Nyssa plenty to do and Sutton superbly plays the two lookalikes differently. It also defines the moment when I became "a fan" — and a fan of Sarah Sutton as much as Peter Davison.

Some years later, and by that point a professional magazine editor with a leading sci-fi magazine in my portfolio, I finally met her in person. It was at the 2007 London Film and Comic-Con where she graciously agreed to join us on the SFX stand for a day. I'm sure that was the reason why it was so well staffed by SFX team members that Saturday. Ever the professional, I managed to reveal nothing of my childhood crush on her character… right up until the end of the day when my carefully cultivated cool finally broke and I begged for an autograph.

Now if I can just figure out where my penchant for wearing maroon velvet jackets comes from.

Debbie Chazen
Actress
Played Foon Van Hoff in Voyage of the Damned

After I worked with Russell T Davies in a series called Mine All Mine I got a call from my agent saying he wanted me to be in The Sarah Jane Adventures, which I would have loved. But I asked my agent to make sure that, if I was in that, it wouldn't cancel out the opportunity to be in Doctor Who.

And then I got a message back saying, "Oh, Russell didn't realise you'd like to be in Doctor Who, so he's going to write you into the Christmas episode!" — at which point I fell on the floor and then ran around the room laughing hysterically, because I am a big fan.

I thought it was a great story and a great script. I don't tend to watch things I'm in because it's always quite horrific to see oneself, but I did make an exception on Christmas Day with all the family. It was so exciting — and actually being in an episode was brilliant.

"I had to hug David Tennant and Kylie for 10 minutes."

I think it probably worked in my favour that I hadn't watched much Doctor Who as a kid. The only reason was that it seemed to be so much more of a boy's show — in my household it was all girls, so it wasn't the sort of thing we'd go out of our way to catch. I feel rather sorry about that now because I do think it would have been fun at the time. My late father, Arnold Chazen, was actually in an episode as an extra. It was a black and white story, *The Moonbase*, with Patrick Troughton. Someone I met on set sent me a reel of his performance, which is hysterical, because the character he plays poisons himself and it's the worst acting I've ever seen! One arm is on his chest and one arm is held out and it looks as if he's giving this big aria. It was really funny.

But, I have to say, if you want to know my particular favourite moment of working on Doctor Who, it was the day I had to hug the Doctor and his companion for about 10 minutes in a scene. I think it was David the first day and then Kylie. By that stage, we'd all worked together for a couple of weeks and all got on well as friends. But it was still so surreal because in your head you're thinking, "Oh my God, David Tennant! I'm hugging David Tennant! I'm hugging Kylie!"

Courtland Lewis

Writer, lecturer, philosopher
Co-edited Doctor Who and Philosophy, a study of Gallifreyan ethics

Some of my first memories are of my grandfather and I watching Doctor Who, enthralled by a time-traveling alien with

"I found myself both dumbfounded and excited."

a long scarf, a robotic dog, monsters, and countless other fascinations. These special memories were enhanced the night I first encountered regeneration. While hurrying out of the kitchen, with a milkshake in my hand, to see the weekly PBS broadcast of Doctor Who, I met not one, but five Doctors! At the young age of six I found myself both dumbfounded and excited. "What happened to the Doctor?" My brothers tried to explain, but their words didn't make sense. "Regene-what?" That night, Doctor Who challenged my understanding of life, and of death, and I have never been the same.

And so, Doctor Who and its willingness to push the limits of human understanding enticed me to become what I am today, a lover of wisdom — a philosopher. To me, the Doctor's adventures are an analogy of the search for truth, and regeneration is an analogy of the willingness to give up one's self in light of new discoveries, to be reborn anew with a fresh understanding of the meaning of life, love, relationships, and the good. The Doctor's task became my own, and so I began my own regeneration: to care more, to do more, to be more… like the Doctor.

For the past 20-something years, especially since *The Five Doctors*, Doctor Who has been a constant reminder of the joy one receives from seeking to understand life's mysteries. From Peter Davison escaping Cybermen to Jon Pertwee and Lis Sladen sneaking past the Raston Warrior Robot; from Tom Baker trapped in the time-scoop to meeting the lovable Patrick Troughton for the first time; that night, Doctor Who tossed me into the time vortex that would forever engulf my life.

Rick Wakeman
Musician, composer, keyboard player
Was born in Perivale, the same place as the Doctor's companion, Ace

I think I was about 14 when Doctor Who first appeared on our television screens.

I never liked watching "scary" things usually, but there had been a lot of stuff written about this new series and so I can vividly recall sitting on my own in my parent's tiny dining room waiting for it to come on the screen.

The theme tune was fantastic. Unlike anything else I'd ever heard, especially on television. I thought the police box TARDIS was brilliant but the costumes seemed to have been made by Blue Peter viewers who had never won anything, and the sets were comparable to those on Crossroads!

I think it was around Christmas that the Daleks appeared.

How on earth we took misshapen dustbins with sink plungers attached to them to our hearts, I'll never know, but we did, and I, like millions of others, loved them. (I actually know where one of the originals is at this very moment.)

Sales of sink plungers rocketed in our area and many a school detention was had for holding egg whisks to foreheads and shouting "Exterminate" at various teachers.

"The theme tune was unlike anything I'd ever heard."

Quite a few metal dustbins went missing too.

Since then, I've only watched when the Daleks reappear but not otherwise. Jolly nasty they may be, but they'd still make better MPs than the ones we seem to get.

Jeremy Dyson
Writer
In 1994, created Dandy Lord, a spoof Doctor Who fanzine, with Mark Gatiss

Doctor Who is still a bright star in the firmament of my childhood memories. The earliest recollections are truly spectral — full of fear and awe: my brother being a Dominator, scaring me by talking in a robotic voice; a glimpse of a writhing demon in *The Time Monster*; the Master introducing the Doctor to some "old friends" in the final episode of *Frontier in Space* and me watching in terror as a host of Daleks appeared over the rim of a hill behind him. But the most vivid of all these relates to a real life encounter.

Blackpool, the spring of 1974. I was seven — nearly eight — and the highlight of our stay was a visit to the still-new Doctor Who exhibition. I was, by now, a confirmed Doctor Who fan, owner of the original Piccolo edition of The Making of Doctor Who, all the Target novelisations and the Radio Times 10th Anniversary Special.

I was already in a state of fervent excitement having just visited the famous North Pier joke shop when we arrived at the exhibition entrance which took the form of a TARDIS parked at the side of a building adjacent to Louis Tussaud's waxworks.

Still young enough for the border between what's imagined and what's perceived to be very leaky it felt like I was actually going to enter a space that was bigger on the inside than it was on the outside.

We passed within. The space was dark, the clamour of the Golden Mile immediately diminished, a steep flight of stairs led down. Fear, thrill, joy — all intermingled in a moment of pure intensity as I gripped my mother's hand. And then I heard it, calling from the bottom of the staircase. That familiar electronic vibrating tonality. Speech rendered empty of humanity. The sound of pure terror. I froze.

"Come on," said Mum.

But I couldn't move. Literally. I couldn't take another step towards the actual Dalek I knew patrolled the bottom of that stairwell.

She — and my father — were utterly bemused. I'd been looking forward to this visit for weeks, months even. And now I wouldn't go in. My father had paid already. I assume (but have no memory) that my older brother was there too. So they left me. Left me at the top of the stairs, outside the TARDIS, to wait for them while they got their £1.50 worth. How I wanted to descend. How I wanted to join them and see the glories of the universe displayed beneath the Blackpool pavement. But nothing, no force on Earth would have enabled me to pass that Dalek. Not for the last time in my life, the fear won out, keeping me from the thing I loved the most.

> **"They left me at the top of the stairs, outside the TARDIS."**

Paul Hartnoll

Musician, songwriter, founder member of Orbital
Met Matt Smith by a fridge at a party after the Coachella Festival, California, in 2010

I had my first really intense Doctor Who experience before I'd even been to primary school, probably around the age of three or four. When I was still in that abstract stage. My two favourite things on the television at the time were Doctor Who and Play School. That was it.

We came from Dartford, and I used to have to go and stay with my nan occasionally. The day I remember particularly was one of those affairs where my mum said, "I'm gonna drop you off at your nan's but she's got a nice thing for you to do. There's a fête around the corner and they're having a Dalek and Brian Cant is bringing it." To me, that was explosive news. Brian Cant *and* a Dalek — they were both going to be in the same place and I was too. Not in London or somewhere far away. In Dartford. The Dalek invasion of Dartford! Brilliant. It was beyond the realms of Jim'll Fix It.

We approached the school, and I walked in through the gate. There it was, on the netball court, a full-on, proper Dalek. And next to it was, as promised, Brian Cant...

And he was feeding children to the Dalek!

Literally, he would open the top half, plop a screaming child into it and close the lid. Then they would push it up and down the concrete playground. I absolutely crapped myself! My world came tumbling down. I didn't know things could get this bad. But it was too late for me to ask my nan, "Can you get me out of here? I don't want to be fed to Dalek by Brian Cant." So I stood there like a lemon and just shook in fear. Slowly, very slowly, the queue moved forward and I got closer and closer...

Then the most excruciating thing happened. Brian Cant turned round to look at me, squatted down to my eye level, smiled and said, "Hello, what's your name?"

"Brian Cant was feeding children to the Dalek!"

Aaaargh!

I just flipped out. He'd broken the fourth wall.

Suddenly, I didn't care about the Dalek behind him, waiting to be fed. He wasn't frightening me any more. Brian Cant, pretty much everyone's second dad from the television, talking directly at me was just too much. I screamed and tried to crawl into my nan's coat until I had to be escorted away. I can still remember the look of horror on his face. I don't think a child had screamed at him for years.

The Dalek, I seem to recall, was fairly ambivalent about the whole thing.

Mal Young

Former executive producer of Doctor Who
Developed heat-stroke while pitching the series to Los Angeles TV companies in 2004

We'd tried to bring back Doctor Who on a few occasions. I'd inherited BBC drama series in-house department and I was always looking for what was in the archive. So, from 1997 onwards we chatted about it but the rights weren't ours. Someone who had been at BBC Worldwide for about five minutes had given them away without checking.

But I remember our head of development at the time, Patrick Spence, saying to me, "Russell T Davies. If we were ever to bring back Doctor Who he's gotta be the one because he's a nut for it, a complete obsessive." And, of course, we knew him as a great writer. So we logged that away in the back of our minds. Every year I would go to my boss, Alan Yentob, and ask, "Is there any way we can get back these rights to our own show?"

> **"It was in the DNA of the BBC that Russell had to write it."**

Then, one day, I had a call to say they'd released it. It all fell into place within minutes, literally. Russell got the call because, by this point, it was just in the DNA of the BBC building that he had to write it. No one ever questioned it. And, indeed, his reaction was, "Oh my God, I will clear my desk to do this!"

A big part of working at the BBC, and I mean this quite sincerely, is that it's the only time in your professional life where you will make shows with no agenda other than the pursuit of excellence and truth. That was my job, every day. If I had to save money on Doctor Who, it was to make it go further, not to put it in the pockets of shareholders. That, for a creative, is the best job in the world.

So my favourite memory of the show was that call and what it led to: listening to Russell develop his vision, before even a word was written, and me realising how good that could be.

Julian Glover

Actor

First appeared in Doctor Who playing Richard the Lionheart in The Crusade

I've been playing villains all my life. That's what I do. It started with my very first feature film, Tom Jones, a classic of cinema. That was my first villain, Northernton. I used to play nice people before that. And then of course I did the big ones: Indiana Jones, The Empire Strikes Back and For Your Eyes Only. I've played villains on TV in The Avengers, The Saint and Jason King. I am always the baddie.

So it was almost inevitable that I'd play the cold, expressionless Count Scarlioni in *City of Death*. His name was actually Scaroth, the last of the Jagaroth. He was a creature who existed throughout the whole of history, that was the point of him. He was trying to find another planet for his people to live on. So he came down to Earth and performed various scams along the way, throughout history, including reproducing the Mona Lisa — which he did quite successfully — but then, of course, he was found out.

Then the villain was literally unmasked. In that famous scene at the end of episode one, I had to wear a completely different shirt and a different scarf to cover up my neck. I put my hand down at the bottom and started to pull and then, courtesy of a bit of clever editing, there he was, horrible old Scaroth revealed — a green, worm-covered face with one eye.

> **"Scaroth had a green, worm-covered face with one eye."**

It was all in the studio, except for a sequence in Paris. I didn't get to go to that, which was rather annoying. Several of the others had a very nice three-day trip to Paris along with Tom Baker and Lalla Ward. Even Tom Chadbon, who didn't have a very large part in the story, was over there because he played the detective who followed them around. I was stuck in BBC Television Centre, thank you very much! Although I was with the divine Catherine Schell — lucky girl — playing my wife. And with a story as well-written as *City of Death*, which itself has become a sort of cult… well, then you get noticed a lot.

Jonathan Ross

TV and radio presenter
Once asked Matt Smith where the hot tub is in the TARDIS

The Doctor Who stories I used to love best — and still do — were the ones that happened on Earth, more or less in contemporary times. Even though it was clearly for budgetary reasons, it was kind of brilliant to see the Doctor and the monsters fighting it out in Acton High Street. The juxtaposition between the strange and the commonplace stuck in my mind: extraordinary people in ordinary places. You'd have this man from space, acting as an advisor to the British army in UNIT, and they'd be riding around in jeeps near slagheaps. You had to check the local quarry to make sure they weren't really there.

Those images of the everyday lasted longest. As a young boy, I remember seeing the Cybermen walk down some steps outside St Paul's Cathedral and it being absolutely terrifying. The way they marched, and the way they moved, ever so slowly: wave after wave of them coming, and nothing much you could do to stop them, because they just didn't care. Despite the hive mind thing going on, you knew they were still individuals. They seemed like really creepy, clever people. It's the same sort of nihilism you see in zombie movies, the bleakness of it all. At least with the Daleks you believed you could wind them up into making the wrong decision. No such luck with Cybermen.

As I got older, I was exposed to slightly more mature, more sophisticated science fiction. I started to go to comic conventions, getting into horror, anime, manga, animation, but — while I was off reading stuff like Frank Herbert's Dune — for Doctor Who, that time seemed to coincide with the more flamboyant excesses of the BBC wardrobe department. By the end of Tom Baker's era I was watching the show purely because of the performance — he

> **"The Cybermen seemed like really creepy, clever people."**

brought all of the whimsy and depth of character to the role that perhaps later only went into the costumes.

Go to a sci-fi convention and you'll see plenty of those costumes. Ordinary people in extraordinary outfits. In 1986, about the time the Watchmen comics first came out, I saw a young boy dressed as Tom Baker, sonic screwdriver in hand. That was quite bold, because people just didn't do it then. But last year, I met one wearing the full David Tennant costume; plimsolls, trench coat, the blue suit underneath it, the lot. Then I met another, dressed exactly the same. Then another, and another, wave after wave, marching slowly towards me, and suddenly I felt like there was nothing I could do to stop them.

You see, when you get to my age, the memories tend to meld together a little bit, that's the problem.

Angellica Bell
TV presenter
Queued to get Colin Baker's autograph at Texas Homecare in 1985

If you'd asked me a couple of years ago if I considered myself a die-hard Doctor Who fan, I'd have said no. But I realised recently that it must have somehow got under my skin. The way it's plotted nowadays, you can't get away with watching just the one episode. When Matt Smith's series started I caught the first one and was slowly, very gently roped in to it. It's so cleverly written, you have to pay attention. There's no point trying to answer emails, or tweet at the same time.

And then, one day, I was out shopping and I saw a blue police box in an antiques shop. It wasn't actually the full-sized prop, it was a wardrobe — but I found myself thinking, "Oh, I really want that for my son." It just looked so iconic. I immediately rushed off home to see where I could put it in the house.

When I went back... of course, it had gone. Obviously, it had dematerialised to another world.

However, my favourite memory of Doctor Who is the day I was told I had to keep a really big secret. For three years I co-presented children's television with Andrew Hayden-Smith. I knew, when he joined, he was an actor and heartthrob — he'd been in Byker

Grove for years — but when he was cast in Doctor Who, that was a big moment.

I also know Noel Clarke very well too, who ended up playing two parts alongside him in *Rise of the Cybermen*. There were major ripples through the CBBC production team. It was massive. Doctor Who had come back so spectacularly and was on the rise, and now the guy that I spent every afternoon with live on BBC1 was going to be rubbing shoulders with the big-wigs in Cardiff.

> "There were major ripples through the CBBC production team."

It was completely hush-hush but Andy and I are really close, so he told me. It wasn't until the news got out later that I realised how huge it was. Now he's part of the Who canon. I think he's been really cool about it, really down to earth. Yet, now he calls me up and says, "Hey, I'm off to Chicago to do a signing at a convention." It is really weird to see people flocking around him in LA and Orlando, asking him for his autograph.

Hey, who needs a TARDIS when the show can take you all over the world like that?

Marc Platt
Author
Wrote Ghost Light, *the final story of Sylvester McCoy's era to go into production*

My parents' lives changed radically on 23 November 1963. From that fateful day, they had to endure a son with an obsession — a 10-year-old whose future life would be indelibly marked out in Saturday night episodes, the way other people give you directions marked out by public houses. Inevitably there were also episodes I missed, but I still remember them too.

28 March 1964. *Marco Polo*, episode three. Easter holidays mean a week in a holiday bungalow at Pevensey Bay. And no TV!

22 August 1964. *The Reign of Terror*, episode three. Friends are staying. Dad insists we take the dog for a walk!

12 February 1966. *The Massacre of St Bartholomew's Eve*, episode two. In detention at school for some forgotten crime. I was a dayboy at boarding school, which meant school on Saturdays. Didn't tell parents about the detention. They probably thought I was growing out of Who.

2 September 1967. *The Tomb of the Cybermen*, episode one. Travelling by car from a holiday in North Wales. At five o'clock we are still on the M1, the TV is in Eastbourne and I'm still kidding myself we'll get home in time.

"My parents' lives changed radically on 23 November 1963."

30 March 1968. *Fury from the Deep*, episode three. Visit family friends and get dragged to a football match! Heaven knows who was playing, but it must have run late. At 5.15pm-ish, I pretend to go to the loo hoping there's a TV under the stands — no such luck.

2 November 1968. *The Invasion*, episode one. A bad year this. For my mum's birthday treat, we drive to Brighton to see newly reissued Gone with the Wind. Not impressed. Even missing episode one, I know that Scarlett O'Hara and Rhett Butler are no match for Tobias Vaughn.

29 January 1972. *The Curse of Peladon*, **episode one**. Megaexcitement as Radio Rentals delivers our first colour TV today. Then I have a mega-row with my dad and he bans me from watching Doctor Who. I was 18 for God's sake! I think I'm still wounded by this.

My dad died the day I had to hand in the final draft script of *Ghost Light*. He wouldn't have known about it anyway. By 1989 he was in a home, suffering from Alzheimer's which, allied to profound deafness, had severed him from reality totally.

He had no idea who I was, but months earlier I'd given him the first script draft to hold. That was just for me really — a way of saying thank you. But not knowing any better, he took the script and did what he always did with anything new.

He tried to eat it.

Charlie Higson

Author, actor, comedian
Composed an entire broadsheet article mistakenly
crediting the revival of Doctor Who to Russell Grant

Doctor Who was one of those things that was there right though my childhood, right up to the departure of Tom Baker really. As a piece of television, it was always interesting to me, particularly the way it went through different styles and changes depending on the level of budgets they had, the length of series and, of course, the different Doctors and writers.

I was always a big fan of science fiction. In my teenage years I read a lot of it and Doctor Who was the closest thing on TV. It wasn't always "hard" sci-fi but I liked it when it was dealing with challenging ideas. They had some very ideas-driven writers, such as Douglas Adams, even then.

What I find fascinating about science fiction is very much how it can be used as satire on what is going on now, by taking it to fantastic extremes. You saw that, to some extent, with a lot of what Russell T Davies contributed in his scripts. At the same time, he married that with his interest in popular drama and soap opera. It's a kids' programme. It had to be understandable at that level. That's why the reboot was such a success, because there was the science stuff for the nerds, there was the social satire to give it a bit of bite and there was the soap opera stuff, with Rose and her family, which got the mass audience — the female audience that's vital for a popular drama. I think he was very clever.

> **"It's a kids' programme. It has to be understandable at that level."**

The great achievement is being able to deal with all these aspects without people realising. One of the things that I discovered when I was asked to write an introduction to Doctor Who and The Crusaders was — and this was a story from one of the very early series — that the show was set up to be educational for children. The first two assistants were Susan's teachers, one a history teacher and the other a science teacher. The idea was that stories would alternate between historic episodes, where they would travel back in history and look around, and episodes that dealt with science. The teachers were there to explain it all. Of course, when they got up and running, that side of it sort of fell away and the show took on a life of its own.

As I have found with my own writing, to maintain a popular, recurring character you've got to have a kit of components that you can keep reusing. In Doctor Who, you can change the Doctor himself; you've got the TARDIS; you've got Daleks; you've got the assistants. As long as you've got that kit, and that kit is a good strong kit, you can keep remaking it forever.

Jason Arnopp

Journalist and author
As a child, became convinced the Master was real and still isn't 100% sure

I knelt on the ATMOS factory's loading bay floor. A UNIT soldier loomed over me, training her rifle at my head. UNIT's medical officer Martha Jones strode past nearby, as the Doctor and Donna Noble looked on.

Thanks to a schedule change and a temporary shortage of extras, I'd found myself in an episode of Doctor Who, namely 2008's *The Sontaran Stratagem*. Having been skulking around, covering the set for Doctor Who Magazine, I was whisked away for a costume change and beard shave. While no Sontarans were involved with my one scene, I was flabbergasted to suddenly be yanked into a fictional world I'd worshipped since I was four.

> **"I'd found myself in an episode of Doctor Who."**

As director Douglas Mackinnon requested take after take, I tried not to get too "method" about my performance. My character was a nameless factory drone. He barely even existed. He certainly had no back story whatsoever. No point in even thinking about that sort of thing...

Raphael Goodship was born in Lowestoft, Suffolk to an Israeli chess champion and a Scottish docks worker. He was an unruly schoolboy and an inveterate stealer of pens. At the age of 28, he robbed and ate various rare breeds of fish from a Beccles gardening centre and was sentenced to four years in prison, during which time he broke the world record for stitching together the most trousers in a 72 hour period and wrote his autobiography, entitled Pens, Fish & Trousersmithery. Once freed, he joined ATMOS. A suspicious Raphael conducted his own daring investigation into the factory's satnav products, only to be captured, killed and cloned by Sontarans.

All Doctor Who fans are blessed with a heightened imagination. It's one of the show's many gifts. I was so excited about my role as Raphael Goodship's Clone, that shortly afterwards I got on the wrong train and ended up in Swansea rather than London.

Adam Hussain
Member of Welsh rap assassins, Goldie Lookin Chain
Made a pact with bandmate Grayham the Bear to collect every Doctor Who DVD ever released

For my first date with my girlfriend, I took her to the Maenllwyd Inn, between Cardiff and Newport. I was having dinner with her and she was telling me all about herself — the things that she likes and all that. I was trying to be impressive and interesting but all of a sudden I could hear this voice behind me and I was thinking, "That sounds pretty familiar".

So I turned around... and it was Colin Baker!

I was like, "Oh my God!" I immediately stopped speaking to her and started talking to Colin Baker instead. Oh, the questions I wanted to ask him. I could have sat down with him for the rest of the afternoon but I thought, "No, keep him nice and sweet."

Between me and you, though, when *The Trial of a Time Lord* came on I was completely lost, I didn't have a clue what was going on. I watched the first one, *The Mysterious Planet* — I think that was the name — and when it cut to the courtroom I was thinking, "What the hell?" Fortunately, Peri got me through those years, if you know what I mean? Wink wink, nudge nudge.

I've got loads of favourites, all the classics; *Earthshock*, *Horror of Fang Rock*, *The Caves of Androzani*. I quite like *Remembrance of the Daleks* as well, because it's freaky. It's got that girl in it — it's all a bit too "in your living room" for me and that's a bit unnerving, but I loved the idea of it. With that, and *Survival* and *Battlefield*, there were a lot of stories built or set around modern-day Britain at that time, but they were bringing back characters from past eras, to join forces.

> ## "I tried to get the missus into Doctor Who. She wasn't having any of it."

Bringing people together, that's what it's all about. I've tried to get the missus into it — yeah, she's still going out with me. I was trying to impress her with the Autons the other day, but she wasn't having any of it.

I watched *The Talons of Weng-Chiang* with her. It's my absolute favourite. There's a part in that where they rip Magnus Greel's mask off, and he's got this horrible, deformed face. As a kid, I thought that was the coolest thing I'd ever seen in all my life. I was absolutely petrified! But, you know, that's all part and parcel of it. I enjoyed being scared… I couldn't believe that they were putting it on at six o'clock in the evening.

Caroline Morahan
Actress, model, TV presenter
Appeared in Alternate Empire, a "conceptual mash-up" of Doctor Who and Star Wars

My earliest Doctor Who memory finds me hiding behind the chocolate leather sofa of my parents' first home, using my "blanky" as a defence against the dreaded Daleks. Tom Baker was still manning the TARDIS and I should have been in bed.

> ## "I became the Doctor's assistant!"

My dad was a huge fan. I had crawled into the living room unnoticed while he watched, transfixed by the on-screen action. He even had his own Doctor Who scarf — a seemingly endless affair in dark orange and yellow wool that must have made riding his bicycle to work a high-risk endeavour.

In retrospect, the Doctor's adventures were perhaps a little advanced for a pre-schooler. I can without doubt attribute a childhood nightmare or two to the life-size salt cellars that bellowed their dreaded war cry: "Exterminate! Exterminate!"

But my interest was piqued.

Soon after, I fell in love with the Time Lord's next incarnation: Peter Davison. In my eyes, the blond Doctor looked like a grown up version of the Milky Bar kid — who I was dead set on marrying. I loved the limitless possibilities of his adventures but remained petrified of the Daleks.

Now that I'm a grown up I find things didn't quite turn out as planned. I'm not married to the Milky Bar kid, or living in a house made out of white chocolate. However, another fantasy of mine has been realised: I became the Doctor's assistant! Sort of…

Shortly after moving to Los Angeles from Dublin, my manager sent me in to audition for a web series. The ambitious project was written and produced by the multi-talented Julian Bane — a Doctor Who fanatic with expert knowledge on all things Gallifreyan. To my delight (and also my dad's), I booked the job.

I've since travelled the galaxies, had run-ins with the Krall and been taken hostage by Sith. Never a dull moment! Look it up on YouTube and you can join in the antics.

Kim Lakin-Smith

Author
Aunt's claim to fame is that Timothy Dalton, Rassilon in The End of Time, *played piano at her house*

Cybernetics is a dominant theme in many of my stories and the gruesome Davros is uniquely responsible. For me, there's something fascinatingly macabre about his combination of flesh and metal. Perhaps it's the reminder of just how vulnerable the human body really is, or fear that, once encased in a skin of metal, we all have the capacity to lose our compassion, mercy and kindness… our *humanity*, in other words.

Writer Terry Nation knew exactly what he was doing when he channelled this deep seated fear of the cyborg into Doctor Who's most enduring enemy, the Daleks. But while a seven-year-old me could cope with a Dalek's mechanical appearance, Nation's masterstroke was to saw open that tin can and lever back the lid, revealing Davros — their creator.

"A cross between a dried-up walnut and a 1970s DJ rig."

Watching the 1979 four-parter *Destiny of the Daleks*, I considered Davros the ultimate bogey man. From the waist up, this crazed scientist looked unnervingly human. But, ghoulishly, Davros had taken apart his own body, cell by cell, to create a self-spawned master race. The eyes too, those windows onto the soul, were stitched up and replaced with one cybernetic orb. Davros's lower half, meanwhile, was hidden inside the life-support chair which inspired the design of his precious Daleks.

A bastardised cross between a dried-up walnut and a 1970s DJ rig, Davros was not just visually terrifying. He was also given to bouts of violent exclamation like a sadistic Screech Owl. Rarely has a character enjoyed such fascist megalomania — or such pantomime baddy banter with Tom Baker's exuberant Fourth Doctor.

By combining Davros's repulsive appearance and voice with the personality of a hypoglycaemic Nazi, Nation created a Doctor Who villain to haunt children for eternity. I, for one, have never recovered.

Michael Underwood

TV presenter
Was sorely tempted to steal a knob from the TARDIS console during a live broadcast from Cardiff

My favourite memory of Doctor Who is reporting on the star-studded press launch party of David Tennant's second series, held in the Crystal Room of the May Fair Hotel in London. For two reasons.

Firstly, the scale of it struck me. I knew that the BBC were really proud of Doctor Who, but I hadn't realised that they would go to such lengths to celebrate it. It was a big room, in a big hotel, with big stars and, I imagine, an even bigger bar tab. No expense was spared. All the cast and crew were there, and all the press and media. I just remember being totally sucked into the hype. It was such a massive event, like being at a movie premiere. They gave out popcorn to eat when we watched the two episodes, *Smith & Jones* and *The Shakespeare Code*. They had the Daleks there, and the TARDIS, right in the middle of the room. There was even an overspill screening area for people who couldn't make it into the main cinema.

I really liked the fact that they'd made such a big deal of it. I was also really excited about meeting Freema Agyeman for the first time. There was a lot of kerfuffle — and I don't use that word very often — around her casting and how that would work. Billie Piper had obviously been such a big success, there was a feeling that Freema had very big shoes to fill. So I was really looking forward to interviewing her, and, of course, I was pleasantly surprised. She was lovely. Quite naturally, too, she was awfully concerned about what people thought of her.

> "It was a big room, in a big hotel, with big stars, and an even bigger bar tab."

I felt they had to make those first couple of episodes big, for her. They had to make an impact, otherwise there was a risk of people slating her. It was very hard trying to be professional that night as, although I was there to cover the launch — I was on duty and my producer was there — I really wanted to "geek around". But I never did get the photo (which surely everyone wants) of me standing in the doorway of the TARDIS.

Here's the second thing, though.

Almost exactly four years later, when my wife and I were looking for wedding reception venues — we knew we wanted to have it in central London — I do remember thinking, "I seem to recall a really great room for an event in Mayfair". Subconsciously, I must have associated good feelings with that place, because that's where we decided to have our party.

Shh! Don't tell her.

Jo Whiley

DJ and television presenter
Interviewed Matt Smith in front of a crowd at the
Westfield shopping centre

Doctor Who has always been a real family passion. I used to go round to my grandparents' house to watch it on their TV. That's where I first saw the Sea Devils, and the Sontarans (who I was frightened of at first but gradually began to think of as quite funny-looking). The only episode I've not seen since is Paul McGann's movie, so I should probably dig that out.

I've never been embarrassed about being a fan. I can talk about Doctor Who until the cows come back to wherever they come. My sister Frances, on the other hand, used to be absolutely obsessed with it. She has learning difficulties and would get terribly upset whenever the characters were in danger. Those weekly cliffhangers were a nightmare. She adored Tegan and Turlough, though, so, in 1983, we were all packed off in the car to Longleat's Doctor Who Celebration and dutifully had our photos taken with the TARDIS and the cast.

Then, for me, it was off to college in Brighton. Doctor Who wasn't particularly cool at the time — but then neither was I — so I joined the local Doctor Who Appreciation Society. You may not be surprised to hear that I was the only girl there. We used to go round to each other's houses and watch old episodes — fourth-generation VHS dubs pirated from Australian television — and that's where I saw my first Patrick Troughton story.

It's still a family thing. My daughter India loves the Sylvester McCoy stories. When I worked on The Word, for some reason we had a Dalek backstage and so I made sure she had her photograph taken with it, hands clasped over her ears, screaming. The one thing I think people forget is that it still wasn't cool when it came back with Christopher Eccleston. I used to mention it on my Radio 1 show but it wasn't until the end of the first series that people started to notice. Obviously the production team were

> **"We used to watch fourth-generation VHS dubs of old episodes."**

listening, though, because soon the invites arrived to take the kids to visit the studios and attend the press launches.

My son Jude was so frightened at the preview screening of *The Shakespeare Code* that I had to take him out of the cinema and into the lobby. Russell T Davies was there, taking a break outside so we went to talk to him. He was lovely but I realise now that he probably thought this was a good opportunity to do a bit of market research. He asked Jude what his favourite monsters were, and I asked him if he was planning to bring my favourites, the Sontarans, back. He said "We'll see…"

And he smiled.

Conor McNicholas

Journalist, former editor of the NME
Was rendered paralysed with fear by a photo of Davros on the cover of the Radio Times in 2008

When Tom Baker fell from Jodrell Bank radio telescope and regenerated as Peter Davison it felt, to the eight-year-old me, to be a moment of monumental significance. It was the death and rebirth of my hero; my own version of the Christ story being played out; the end of a special era.

Looking back, the transfer said everything about the death of the crazy 1970s and the birth of a more straight-laced 1980s. Mrs Thatcher might have taken over as Prime Minister in 1979 but it took the Doctor's fourth regeneration to really send the message that things would never be the same again. Gone was cuddly uncle Tom Baker with his unkempt curly mop and flowing scarf, his coat of many colours, wry wit and swirling undercurrent of darkness. In his place came Peter Davison in altogether more respectable cricket garb, the cream trousers and starched shirt uniform of the establishment. You can bet that under the v-necked jumper was a pair of red braces…

"Books became my route to the Doctor."

I pined for the real Doctor, the Tom Baker Doctor, immediately. Something had been lost and the impostor left in his place didn't do justice to the character I'd grown up with. As a result I threw myself into the books. When I stayed with my dad, every other weekend, I'd spend hours in Clayton village library living out the early Baker-years episodes I'd missed, all pyramids on Mars and android invasions. Plastic-covered hardback books by Terrance Dicks became my route to the Doctor I sought. I can still smell the fusty aroma of those browning pages, sweet but decaying like a ripe dessert wine.

Equally, Tom Baker continues to fascinate. For me and my circle of friends, he'll always be the Doctor whether he likes it or not, and every single thing he does — every time he's spotted drinking in the Coach and Horses in Soho, every expletive-laden voice-over out-take that's leaked on the internet — is dissected over a pint with love and admiration.

Jacqueline Rayner
Writer
Was banned from watching Doctor Who in 1979 after it made her develop a fear of bathroom lights

2004. Eight years since the TV Movie, and a year before *Rose* would hit the screens. But the world wasn't entirely without new Doctor Who — a missing episode had been found!

"The clip cut away just as a mysterious figure appeared."

The recovery of Day of Armageddon, episode two of *The Daleks' Master Plan* was reported on the BBC News. They showed a clip, and that was jolly exciting, of course, but at the end… Aaaargh! The clip cut away just as a mysterious figure appeared, silhouetted at the top of a walkway. I turned to my husband. "Was that… was that… a *delegate*?!"

It seemed astonishing to me that this, the first live action appearance of a Dalek delegate (aka a Planetarian) on British telly for 38 and a bit years wasn't actually the lead story. Could it be that the people in charge of BBC News didn't realise what a big deal this was? Where was the red button service devoted to coverage of newly rediscovered minor science fiction characters?

Luckily we'd been recording the news because a report seemed likely, so I was able to watch that less-than-a-second arrival of the alien I knew to be named Zephon about a billion times.

Yes, I am that sad.

Wonderfully, the BBC Cult web team fairly quickly put up a "photo-novel" of screen grabs, and I looked at that a billion times too.

Stills of the delegates — woooo! Pictures of Katarina that weren't the same few shots we'd been seeing for donkey's years – yayyy! Steven in his mysterious, where-did-it-come-from jacket. All fab.

And, eventually, I was lucky enough to watch the episode itself. In fact, I think, following its inclusion in the Lost in Time DVD box set, Day of Armageddon is the Doctor Who episode I've seen the most number of times by far.

But that moment, watching the news in my tiny South London flat, was never quite beaten. The fraction of a second when something that had seemed lost forever was suddenly there in front of me. Wow.

David Hankinson

Actor
Was a Dalek operator on Doctor Who from Bad Wolf *to* Journey's End

Let me tell you about the time I fell in love with Doctor Who. It happened during the 17th season, when I was nine years old. I had been well aware of the show before then and we had spent quite some time together, but something special happened between us during those five transmitted stories.

That particular series of Doctor Who so amused and charmed me that, by the end of its run, we were very definitely an item. The 17th season eloquently expressed something which, deep down, I must have felt instinctively: the idea that individuality, spontaneity and a good sense of humour — the chief weapons of the show's heroes — are things to hold very dear. As the Doctor and Romana bamboozled, wrong-footed and destabilised their opponents,

I laughed out loud, relieving my tension as I willed them to escape the clutches of Davros, Adrasta or Soldeed.

The 17th season winked at me, with its continual references to books and plays and art, letting me know that there was a big world out there just over the horizon and that if, like the Doctor and Romana, I was open to it, there was a universe of knowledge and experience waiting to be discovered. The 17th season was built on beautiful ideas — neat ideas, vivid ideas — that always offered up not only monsters but also wildly different consequences arising from their presence: opposing armies whose cold logic had locked their battle computers in eternal stalemate;

> **"By the end of its run, we were very definitely an item."**

a monster trapped on Earth who planned to fund his escape by forcing Leonardo Da Vinci to paint multiple Mona Lisas; a monster that wasn't a monster at all but a wronged and rather irate trade envoy; monsters made of such substance that they were yet more monstrous when dead; cunning monsters that conned you, then killed you.

Amusing, charming, beautiful. What could I do but surrender?

Looking back, I can begin to understand how these elements came together to make something very, very special. At the time, of course, I couldn't explain any of it. I just knew it felt right, like being in love.

Chris Donald
Founding editor of Viz comic
Used the family music centre to record his own comedy versions of Doctor Who and Grandstand in 1975

Patrick Troughton will always be the Doctor for me and he seemed to come up against a stream of classic monsters in the late 1960s — Daleks, Cybermen, Abominable Snowmen, Ice Warriors. As far as I was concerned there was a simple formula for a successful series — locate it on Earth, in the present day, and have an army of monsters wandering about the place, perplexing the authorities. Stick with that and you couldn't go wrong.

I wasn't much into sci-fi — space, time and all that malarkey. It could get a bit silly. Low points for me were people sitting around on a floor chanting "Om-marni-om-inoo", or words to that effect — something to do with a spider? — and a giant prawn chasing people up the stairs in a lighthouse. Then there was that egg headed thing with six arms, a big eye and a voice like Miss Piggy.

"Stick to the bloody formula!" I'd shout at the telly.

I bought a Dalek in 1995, but soon I realised it was a bit of a cliché — making a few bob and buying yourself a Dalek. Pop stars seemed to do it. So I decided to buy a few more — get an invasion force together. I reckoned they'd look great stored in a darkened garage somewhere. I started bidding for them on eBay one night after I'd had a few drinks. I think I was bidding for three or four at the same time. Luckily there were other drunken Doctor Who fans out there with more money than me, and I only bought one more. A red one. I sold that on to a collector in Nottingham. My wife was glad to see the back of it, 'cos they're a bugger to dust.

> **"It was a bit of a cliché, making a few bob and buying yourself a Dalek."**

The bloke in Nottingham has a conservatory with about a dozen Daleks in it. I don't think he's married.

Chantel Shafie

Actress, model, TV presenter
Portrayed Tegan on the box cover of the Dekker TARDIS play tent in 1982

Doctor Who found me when I was three years old. As a child model, I spent a day playing his female companion, in a replica lilac air hostess' outfit. It was one hell of a day!

Before we went to the studio, I decided my handkerchief was too creased. When my mother left the room, I proceeded to accidentally run a hot iron straight over my little hand. I also had whooping cough and a rotten cold, so I remember being in a terrible mood… and it shows in the photos. Directors are always warned against working with animals and children. This was one of those days for him. If you've ever wondered why tiny Tegan looks crotchety on the front of the TARDIS playhouse, it wasn't method acting.

"I spent many a happy day sitting in 'my TARDIS'."

Years later, while at college in London, I saw the boxed toy for sale in the window of a specialist collectors' shop. At £75, it was way too expensive for me to buy. To this day, though, I regret walking by, as I can't find one anywhere now, and they are quite sought after. Much to my dismay, my mother threw mine away after it had literally fallen to pieces!

Nevertheless, I spent many a happy childhood day sitting in "my TARDIS", and am still proud to have been part of Doctor Who… even if it was only in the smallest way possible.

Jack Thorne
Screenwriter and playwright
Collected a BAFTA with Doctor Who producer Caroline Skinner for their supernatural thriller, The Fades

I'm part of the lost generation of Doctor Who.

I was born in December 1978. Peter Davison left the role when I was six, so I got Colin Baker and — you know — Sylvester McCoy, and even he only lasted until I was 10. I thought the show was awful and so concentrated my attention elsewhere. (Since you ask — the animated series of Dungeons & Dragons, May to December, starring the great Anton Rogers, and an occasional dose of 'Allo 'Allo.) Then came the revamp…

I watched it.

Because I watch everything on TV, because I really, really like TV, and because I work in TV. But I didn't expect to like it too much. I remember thinking, with a writer's brain, at the end of *Rose*, "Well, that was impressive. Didn't love it, but, you know, it was impressive." I kept on watching as much because I thought I should than because I wanted to.

I don't think it was just Captain Jack — though his entrance was spectacular. I don't think it was just the gas mask faces — though they were brilliant. I don't think it was just the exceptionally brilliant performance by guest star Florence Hoath as Nancy. (What's she done since? She really should have done more — she's awesome.)

"At the age of 26, I became a die-hard fan of a kids' show."

It was… Well, it was the all of it.

It was the fact that the monsters were invisible; it was the fact that the reality of the orphan kids was so brutal; it was the Chinatown twist that she was his mummy; and it was the fact that it all turned out brilliant in the end.

Some people seem to have forgotten Christopher Eccleston's Doctor — but the joy in his "Just this once, everybody lives" still gives me goosebumps to this day.

The Empty Child and *The Doctor Dances* made me love Doctor Who. And, at the age of 26, I became a die-hard fan of a so-called kids' show.

Gareth Jones
TV presenter, formerly known as Gaz Top
Told Tom Baker he was an Altarian from Altair IV in the foyer of a hotel in Leeds

My dad liked his gadgets. He owned a TV and radio shop so we had a colour telly when most of the people on our road didn't. We were the only early adopters in North Wales! We watched a lot of TV — it was paying for the family's mortgage.

"We'd love to know more about the TARDIS."

Patrick Troughton was always my favourite Doctor. Then I wondered to myself the other day: is he still my favourite Doctor? It's close, you know, because I really, really, like Matt Smith's Doctor. I think he's brought the eccentricity back and, in some ways, I think he's channelling a bit of Patrick Troughton. There's something about the tweediness and the bow-tie-ness; the eccentricity in the eyes is a bit of Troughton.

I like the mischief. I think if you have the ability to travel through space and time you would be a little bit mischievous because you could always fix it if you needed to.

When the Doctor regenerates and this new person appears where does that pattern come from? Who is that person that appears? Are we missing someone else in the universe? Did someone blink out of existence who was, for example, just like Matt Smith but not a Doctor? I'd love to know. There's a consequence there, an area you could exploit in a story, even.

The universe has to balance itself out: for every action there's an equal and opposite reaction. Apply that rule to the Weeping Angels — somewhere in the universe there have to be Laughing Devils. We've had devils, plenty of them, but for the Doctor to be caught in a war between Laughing Devils and Weeping Angels mightn't be a bad premise for a story… if ever I was to write one.

One thing I don't think has ever properly been explained is the origin of the TARDIS: how it works; what's really going on; why it's alive; why it communicates telepathically — all those things. I thought the one episode that had a stab at it, *The Doctor's Wife*, was the best. Neil Gaiman did a great job. It's such a rich vein; we'd love to know more about the TARDIS. We already know lots about the Doctor and, naturally, a story is always going to be an emotional journey… but I like the technology — the vehicles, the weapons, the gadgets. The hardware's very much where I'm at in Doctor Who. I suppose I am my father's son.

Boyd Hilton

TV and reviews editor at Heat magazine
*Mounted a blistering 10-point defence of Doctor Who
against attack by Channel 4 News' culture editor in 2011*

One of the loveliest nights of my life was watching The X Factor final in a hotel room in Cardiff with Russell T Davies, his partner, Matt Lucas and a few other people.

I was, at the time, working with Matt and David Walliams on a Little Britain book, and Russell happened to be good friends with Matt. So he came over to see us and we all had a great, sociable night.

I love Russell's fondness for pop culture. He immerses himself in TV, and he loves these sorts of programmes, which makes it brilliant fun watching with him. I think the winner that year might have been Steve Brookstein — and you must remember how terrible he was — so I had Matt and David making fun of him on one side, and Russell, this funny, engaging, completely lovable bloke, on the other.

In the very, very early days of Heat magazine, he made his break-through series, Queer as Folk, for Channel 4, and I remember going along to the press conference. And, of course, he was getting all these awful questions from the Daily Mail — in that period they were still referring to Michael Grade as the channel's pornographer-in-chief. So he was bombarded with vitriol by the tabloids about how horrible this series was, with these gay people having sex. I think I asked the only question which wasn't down that alley, which didn't talk about how "controversial" it all was. Years later, Russell wrote notes for the re-release of the DVD, and he remembered that one question. I thought that was a really nice thing for him to do.

Subsequently, I wrote about — and championed — everything he did: The Second Coming, Bob and Rose, all those great, beautifully written series. If Heat was ever going to have a favourite writer, he was the one. So, when it was announced that he was taking over Doctor Who, I just thought that it was the most wonderful thing. The idea that the best, most exciting, contemporary British TV writer would be given the chance to run this brilliant show — one that had been left to wrack and ruin, really — was just perfect.

"If Heat was ever going to have a favourite writer, he was the one."

And the really key moment for me, in the whole revival of Doctor Who, was in that very first episode. The BBC asked us, "Can we have a special cover of Heat for Doctor Who?" and we said, "Sure!" But even I didn't know it was going to actually appear in Rose until a couple of days beforehand. Seeing that made it feel so personal. Watching that first episode still, I think it was an absolutely historic piece of television. It was clever, it was well made, the dialogue was funny and it was just, absolutely fun. He didn't let us down at all.

Tom Goodman-Hill

Actor
Developed an obsession with ruffle-fronted shirts thanks to David Bowie and Jon Pertwee

The episode I was in was a lot of fun. It was *The Unicorn and the Wasp*. I was the wasp. The title role — can't be unhappy with that! — which, I think, basically ranks me up there alongside the Daleks, right? The Unicorn was Felicity Jones, who's now a superstar, and Felicity Kendal was my mum. I'd never worked with her before, so that was thrilling. Particularly with the name Tom Goodman-Hill. Everyone used to joke I was half Richard Briers!

"Felicity Kendal was my mum."

But I was mostly delighted because I was working with Graeme Harper, who directed one of my all time Doctor Who faves, *The Caves of Androzani*. It was a beautiful week in Wales. We were down at Tredegar House, out on the lawns and there was a freak three or four day heatwave. It really was a very relaxing shoot. A bit of a relief for David Tennant and Catherine Tate too as they were halfway through a massive block of filming.

It was all shot in one fell swoop because of the nature of the story and it was all set in the one location, so we never left the house and the gardens. It was like we were recording an episode of Poirot, a quite nice chamber piece: all of us there, all the time. When the green screen suddenly came out and I was turning into a wasp it felt a bit odd!

The effects were actually very deliberately old school. The transformation to the wasp was incredibly straightforward. Although the wasp itself was a technically brilliant piece of graphics, the rest of it was just a bloody great purple Maglite shining in my face.

When I was little, the most terrifying story to me was *Planet of the Spiders*. I've been scared of spiders ever since. I already had a fairly difficult time with them but when they killed Sarah Jane — or rather, when I thought she was dead — that became a phobia. Hopefully I've done the same for a new generation of kids with wasps.

Paul Whitehouse

Actor, comedian
Remade Doctor Who as an On The Buses skit for BAFTA-winning series Harry & Paul in 2010

I'm a big fan of Matt Smith. Okay, I thought David Tennant was great — and my kids loved him — but I was slightly jealous because he is conventionally very good looking and women fancy him. So I'm predisposed not to like him, whereas Matt Smith has got enough of the geek about him for me not to feel so challenged. Having said that, of course, he is much younger and much better looking than me so I have to deal with that.

Look at Wilko Johnson, the guitarist with Dr Feelgood, circa 1975. I keep saying this to my kids: "Look at him — look! — he looks like Matt Smith!" They won't have it but I'm convinced I'm right

But I genuinely think he's fantastic. For one so young, he's sort of like an old 1960s-style Doctor. He embodies that. Modern-day Doctor Who has a lot in common with those classy, odd, arty series from the 1960s like The Avengers and The Prisoner anyway. I think it's regained that "classic" feel now — seminal, British, iconoclastic telly that doesn't pander to lowest-common-denominator crash, bang, wallop violence. Which idiot at the BBC cancelled it all those years ago? It's a bone of contention in my life. Who makes those decisions at the BBC? I've worked at the BBC for years and I don't bloody know.

> "When I pop my clogs, the Daleks will be of more significance than Jesus."

It's such an interesting concept, Doctor Who. The Doctor's a pacifist for a start, which is so unlikely for a hero. It's almost as unlikely as Christianity catching on when it did.

Which leads me on to my specific point about Doctor Who — and I'll keep it short and sweet because it is short and sweet — then I'll say no more.

When people have near death experiences, they often say they see a kind of Rolodex of the most vivid moments from their life flashing through their brains. I'm afraid to say that of greater importance than Jesus Christ in my mind will be the Daleks. In that roster of my life, as it whizzes past me and I'm about to pop my clogs, the Daleks will probably be of more significance than Jesus.

Two great imaginary stories and the Daleks win. I think that says enough, don't you?

Anneke Wills

Actress, played the Doctor's companion Polly
Visited the Tenth Doctor in his TARDIS during the filming of Daleks in Manhattan *in 2006*

We need to talk about *The Underwater Menace*.

Why? Because it's very exciting. It's the most exciting thing. A missing episode that has been recently rediscovered but, as you read this, one I haven't yet seen. I want to take the opportunity to reminisce for a final time based solely on my own recollections.

> **"I indignantly shout, 'You're not turning me into a fish!'"**

Now, unfortunately, my overriding memory of this story is that Patrick Troughton was being a bitch to the director, Julia Smith. Sadly, yes, he was making her life hell and it wasn't a great atmosphere in rehearsals. He thought the costumes were silly and the story was stupid.

Now, he may have been right but everybody who has seen it, lucky things, has said — because this is very early on — that you really get a glimpse of how Patrick first played the Doctor, being the clown. I'm really looking forward to revisiting that.

However, more importantly, I want to explain that the rest of the time I had with him — the six months we were on Doctor Who together — were magic days. When we weren't rehearsing, when we weren't just working together, it was heaven to be with him because he was so absolutely, so completely a genuine actor.

He was one of those rare beings. I'll give you a quote by way of example. Alec Guinness said this to Michael Gough: "Now look, dear boy, you have to take your feet off the ground when you're acting. You can't have one foot on the ground like you're in the swimming pool, pretending to swim on the top!"

You have to dive in and Patrick did that for every performance. He dug deep.

In fact, if he hadn't dug so deep and found it within himself to come up with that character, that new Doctor, to carry on where William Hartnell left off, I'm here to tell you we wouldn't still be watching the show today. There wouldn't be any missing episodes, and there certainly wouldn't be celebratory screenings at the BFI when they finally came to light.

I couldn't get up to London in time to see *The Underwater Menace* on the big screen, but a lovely story from the audience did reach me. In one of the scenes they showed (quite frightening for children I think), I'm on a slab and evil scientists are coming at me with a massive great big hypodermic. I'm remonstrating with them and indignantly shout, "You're not turning me into a fish!"

Apparently the whole of the BFI went into a roar of applause.

And do you know what? They still haven't managed to.

Paul Scoones

Writer
Author of The Comic Strip Companion: The Unofficial and Unauthorised Guide to Doctor Who in Comics

It is 1975.

I'm seven years old, sitting on the step that connects the living room at the front of our house to the passage at the rear. Mum comes over and says that she has a book for me.

It is a Doctor Who book, with a man, a dinosaur, a terrifying-looking lizard man and an exploding volcano on the cover.

I know a bit about Doctor Who. It is a mysterious and scary television programme I've recently seen for the first time. Mum likes Doctor Who. She grew up watching the show. It's okay to be scared when Doctor Who is on because she watches with me.

Mum bought the book for herself but after reading thought I might like it. I've never read a book this long before. There are some pictures to help explain things, but most pages just have words and the writing looks tiny.

"It's okay to be scared when Doctor Who is on because my mum watches with me."

On the back of the book, Mum has crossed out a single word with a black felt-tipped pen: "... *Tyrannosaurus rex*, the biggest, most savage mammal which ever trod the earth!" She tells me that whoever wrote that got it wrong — dinosaurs were not mammals.

Mum thinks I should try reading the book by myself. If she thinks I can do it, I must be able to.

I start reading, a chapter a day. I take the book to school. I read it during lunchtime in the classroom on a rainy day while eating my peanut butter sandwiches. The story is enthralling and terrifying in equal measure. I read it through again, several times.

I discover that my local library has other Doctor Who books. I read them all. I'm well and truly hooked...

It is 2010.

I'm now 42 years old, standing in front of a group of mourners who have gathered to remember and say farewell to Mum.

I speak of how she inspired me to set out on the journey that led to where I am now. My life-long fascination with Doctor Who has led to professional work associated with the series. I am a freelance writer, working for the BBC on production notes for the DVDs and writing a book about the comic strips.

And it all started with a book called Doctor Who and the Cave Monsters.

Jason Flemyng

Actor

Went to Mark Gatiss' wedding at Middle Temple in 2008

I have two claims to Doctor Who fame. The first came about because I did a live version of The Quatermass Experiment with David Tennant, who was playing the scientist Doctor Gordon Briscoe.

The day it was announced that he had been cast as the Doctor was the day of the live broadcast, so I very discreetly played up to it. There was a scene about three-quarters of the way through where he walked in and I was meant to say, "Good to have you back with us, Gordon." Instead, I said, "Good to have you back with us, Doctor." So, that's officially the first time on camera he's called the Doctor. That makes it canon. Maybe not officially, but in my head. I'm very proud of it.

The other thing that's technically not official, because I'm sure it would get me into trouble, is the song that we sang to David the same day. It went, to the tune of the old Dusty Springfield number:

"'Cos Eccleston was brilliant but he's got no hair,
It's crazy but it's true, Tennant's playing Doctor Who!"

My second claim to fame resulted in me phoning up Phil Collinson, the producer of the new series when they brought it back. My dad, Gordon, who directed both the Dalek feature films in the 1960s, also provided the noise of the Dalek spaceship. He did the effect himself, and he was the only person alive that could make the take-off sound, but he passed that on to me. So now I'm the only living person, apart from my brother, who can do it.

> **"My dad was the only person alive who could make the Dalek spaceship noise."**

I've got three of the original "Now in Technicolor" Dalek movie posters. They're astronomically expensive but I sort of collect them. (That's my one weird Doctor Who fetish.) They're mostly framed and on the walls but there's a huge cinema one which I have to keep rolled up because it's about 10 metres across.

Anyway, when Doctor Who returned, I phoned up Cardiff and told them I had to talk to the producer. And he said, "No Jason, it's already been cast." I explained, "No, no, no, I don't want to do the part, I want to do the noise of the Dalek spaceship."

And he told me, "But we don't need it, the Daleks fly around by themselves now." So I replied, "This conversation is over. That's the most ridiculous thing I've ever heard!"

Paul Magrs

Writer
Author of, among many other works, The Diary of a Doctor Who Addict

Forton Services is a motorway transport café in the shape of a flying saucer stuck atop a tower. We stopped there for sausage and chips on the way to Blackpool in 1983. It was late October, freezing and blue, and our car reeked of sick from my best friend Michael, who was over-excited. We were all excited, though.

My best moment of Doctor Who isn't even watching it. It's about being in that motorway café and finding the Radio Times 20th Anniversary Special for sale. Reading it in a saucer hovering over the motorway. Getting all excited about the brand new photos of monsters from the past — pictures of things like the Antimatter Beast of Zeta Minor and colour stills of Marco Polo. And learning more about the imminent anniversary story, *The Five Doctors* — or "The Special" as we succinctly called it. We knew that all the old Doctors were coming back. The whole of that 20 years' history seemed crammed into that glossy mag. There was even a pic of the man we knew was going to be the new Doctor, next year. There were glimpses of the stories and monsters still to come — in the unimaginably futuristic year of 1984.

"There were glimpses of monsters still to come."

That same day we still had the Blackpool Doctor Who Exhibition to come — jazzy and tacky, sepulchral, dark — jam-packed with rubber monsters and polystyrene rocks. There was stuffing hanging out of Cybermen, and holes in the yeti's fur, and poor automated K-9 looked as if he hadn't enough room to run around in his paddock, bizarrely filled as it was with the decapitated heads of monsters. But every bit of it was magical.

These were pieces of the true cross, treasures from ancient civilisations, nuggets of gold from the moon. This floppy dinosaur, this fairy liquid spaceship, this TARDIS console looking like a bingo machine. This was the day that Doctor Who seemed more real than anything else in the world.

Hayden Black

Writer, actor, creator of Goodnight Burbank
Missed episode three of The Brain of Morbius *as punishment for fighting with his sister*

I was living in Fort Lauderdale, Florida, having emigrated with my family in the 1980s. I heard that a Doctor Who convention was being held in Miami and I naively decided it would be a great opportunity to meet the producer, John Nathan-Turner, and pass him some of my inchoate scripts.

I found the number for the BBC, called them up, and asked to be put through to the Doctor Who production office. A very British voice sang, "Doctor Who?" and I almost lost my voice. "I'd like to speak to John Nathan-Turner," I managed to reply.

> "To my utter surprise, John Nathan-Turner agreed to meet me."

"Who's calling?"

I could hardly bottom out now. "Hayden Black," I said, realising that, for the first time in my life, my unusual name might be able to open a door. A moment later, he picked up.

I told him — babbled would be more accurate — I was a budding writer and that I'd love to talk to him about my dream job, writing for Doctor Who. To my utter surprise and delight, he agreed to meet me.

The convention arrived. I felt it was professional not to pay the admission price (which would surely tag me as a fanboy) so skipped in and asked someone dressed as an Ogron where I could find John Nathan-Turner. I was ushered to a backstage area where he was waiting with Nicola Bryant to go out and meet his adoring public.

I gave him the large manila envelope stuffed with a handful of sketches then, rather than overstay my welcome, buggered off as quickly as possible.

And that was that.

For a few months.

Until I was back at college, hanging out in someone's dorm room, and my roommate came running in. "Hayden, there's a phone call for you. Sounds long distance". I raced to my room, picked up the phone, and heard none other than John Nathan-Turner. I couldn't believe it. But here was the producer of Doctor Who telling me my sketches weren't bad at all and that if I was interested in writing for the show then I should. "Submit an outline and we'll go from there," he said.

Naturally, I never finished it. I was 19, and easily distracted. Regardless, John Nathan-Turner had reached out, across an ocean no less, and offered unbelievable encouragement to a kid who had a dream. I will be eternally grateful for that. Rest in peace, mate.

Steve O'Brien

Journalist
Used the toilet cubicle next to Matt Smith at the Groucho

In these days of super-dense, arc-hugging TV series, it's occasionally hard to find the point at which you can slip in and enjoy the big story. But Doctor Who's glorious habit of stopping everything to rejuvenate its lead character with a new actor every few years opens it up to curious newbies.

In 1981 I was a fair-weather fan. A Doctor Who Weekly here, a Target novel there, but I'd never done the religious thing with it. However, an impending regeneration meant a new start. Tom

Baker had become the Doctor when I was four. I was too busy with Mary, Mungo & Midge to care back then.

I half-watched the first three episode of *Logopolis* — Jesus H Bidmead's script was just science noise to me. But, come episode four, I was so excited at seeing my first live regeneration that I couldn't sit down, let alone still. I watched the whole episode standing up, not knowing when it would occur. I didn't know that the change-over usually happened at the very end of the story. In fact, there's a bit halfway in, when the Doctor's running and I was sure it was going to happen then, mid-sprint. "He's going to change now, I think!" I'd exclaim every four minutes or so, while Dad peeked witheringly over the top of the local paper, barely bothering to summon fake interest.

"I watched the whole episode standing up."

Oddly, my recollection of the regeneration itself is pretty fuzzy. I've seen it so many times since, I can't separate the repeated viewings from my real first memory of March 1981. But it was the moment that kick-started my bumpy love affair with Doctor Who. To nick a sentiment: after that, Peter Davison was *my* Doctor.

Bernard Holley

Actor
Played an Axon in 1971's The Claws of Axos*, returning to the role in 2011 for an audiobook*

My first Doctor Who job was *The Tomb of the Cybermen*. I was in episode one and killed at the end, so I was a corpse for the whole of the following week. I really decided there and then that being an actor was the life for me. I got paid a full fee for lying dead on the floor and not saying a word!

It's fascinating to watch those old black and white ones, because technology has moved on so fast but, for the time, it wasn't bad, There might be some moments in *The Tomb of the Cybermen* where maybe a handle will wobble a bit, but basically it's all right.

What I like is that the new generation of Doctor Who fans seems to enjoy the old ones as much as the new ones. A neighbour of a friend of mine knows a little boy who is absolutely crazy about Doctor Who. So I sent him a couple of signed photographs. I was told he was completely and absolutely delighted and carries the picture everywhere. I still get youngsters questioning me: "What was it like when you did it?" It's just terrific really. It's nice to be associated with something that's really popular. And I'm still earning money out of these 40-year-old programmes which is really very nice!

In fact, through Doctor Who, I got to know some of the directors who later employed me for occasional jobs — and eventually I was offered a long term contract on Z-Cars. My first Doctor Who led to three and a half years of consistent employment in television.

"The gold paint got everywhere!"

For *The Claws of Axos*, the director, Michael Ferguson, did a great job, too. My abiding memory, unsurprisingly, is being covered in gold. We did four episodes over four weeks, so I had to have the make-up done at some stage or other over each of those weeks. The gold paint got everywhere! Bits and pieces of it kept cropping up in unexpected places for ages after.

There was, at the time, an article in the Radio Times about my "paint job" and I received a very strange letter from a male model who claimed he regularly posed wearing gold and silver. He went into great detail about how he got rid of the paint from his body, from every crack and orifice! Probably the only two people he's ever written to in his life are me and Shirley Eaton.

Daniel Blythe
Author
Mum taught Tom Baker to speak French in 1994

I remember exactly when I first see her, the girl with two names. I'm not allowed to watch "it" at home — too scary, makes me hide behind cushions. But this is Robert's house, with 30 excited five-year-olds packed into the lounge. I am eating cake when the lights go off. A big colour TV springs into life, showing a whooshing blue time-tunnel. And then — *that* music.

I watch carefully, knowing she is important. She gasps for air, recovers. She fades into nothingness on a futuristic couch. Where has she gone? Wait a minute — is that her, in a fancy white tunic, asleep upright inside a plastic casing?

Then, weeks later, scrambling across rocks in a yellow cagoule, gasping "Linx" (which I don't understand)... Then again, this time in mist, pursued by a shadowy figure... She is familiarity; safety, our big sister. She is brave and resourceful, whether inching through ducting this week, standing up to a Sontaran the next, or leading an escape and — "No!" — falling off the scaffolding. The picture, it just froze! More next Saturday...

A generation later, it's still Saturday. My children's favourite Doctor is well into his stride now. (Like mine he has a manic grin, wild hair, an anarchic side. I like him a lot.) He's undercover as a teacher in this story. And into the staff room walks a graceful, middle-aged woman who has stepped out of time. There is no mistaking the glossy hair, dazzling smile and confident sing-song voice. She is back! She is back...

Then... one Easter evening alone with my computer. The family are in Whitby; I am to join them later. Something has happened. Shock and disbelief trickles through on Facebook. Is it true? I'm texting my wife when BBC News confirms it. My eyes sting with tears. I am a middle-aged man sitting at his computer, crying, sobbing. It's a powerful, angry, deep, almost physical pain, wrenched from a place where I am still five years old. Like the death of a sister, of an aunt. It echoes across time from that suburban living-room.

"She was familiarity; safety, our big sister."

I now know she never truly left us. We can watch her over and over again, scurrying through that muddy quarry in a yellow cagoule, squaring up to a pitchfork-wielding Zygon or fearlessly feeling her way across the studio basalt of Karn. We can picture her in dozens of books, hear her voice in audios and in commentaries. If we close our eyes, we can still see her smile.

Goodbye, Sarah Jane. We won't ever forget you.

Rhys Thomas

Actor, writer, comedian, Queen fan
Watched the leaked pilot of Rose *with a friend on a train to Wicklow in 2005*

I loved television growing up. I know there's this view where they say television isn't good for children but I think that's absolutely rubbish. I can't subscribe to the idea that it's a demon because I honestly believe that watching programmes like Doctor Who gave me a vocabulary and an imagination. If you actually pay attention to some of the stories, they're like Shakespearean plays.

I loved Doctor Who even when I was far too young for it. I was only about three or four when it was first transmitted but I remember *Warriors of the Deep* really clearly. I remember every single story from that period.

Then the show was cancelled — just as I was getting obsessed by it. That final series, I thought, with *The Curse of Fenric*, and *Survival*, was really good. But then, there was a lot of excitement in the run up to the 30th anniversary. I remember being very disappointed that there wasn't a new story. I knew this one boy at school, Phillip Taylor, was a fan because he gave me a copy of Doctor Who Magazine. It was 1992, and *The Deadly Assassin* was on the cover, with an archive feature inside. I remember reading about it before I even got it on video because I didn't know the story. It became my favourite at that time.

> "I had a very special suit made up for my stag weekend."

That summer holiday, I spent all my pocket money on Doctor Who videos and Queen albums. This is in the days before UK Gold, there were no repeats, so I had to collect the VHSs. Or I'd go down to the newsagent's every month with my £2.50 and get myself the latest magazine, and I would genuinely not be able to sleep the night before. I even bought the Silva Screen record of the soundtrack music to *The Five Doctors*, although I was disappointed to find that there was no Paddy Kingsland on it.

I think it's safe to say that Doctor Who had an impact.

In 2007, I had a very special suit made up for my stag weekend. I already had the trousers, as it happens, but I needed a jacket. So I went to Paul Smith and asked them to make me a blazer in the same colour and style as the Fifth Doctor's frock coat. It cost about £2,500. My mum asked a lady to knit me a perfect replica of Peter Davison's original cricket jumper. I was very specific that I wanted the first one, not the double red-line pattern from *The Awakening* onward.

Even my daughter now loves the show. She's three and I make her watch it, but she has no interest in the new ones at all. Then again, she hasn't got very good taste, anyway — she likes watching *Dimensions in Time* (I think because there are a lot of old monsters in it). Stick on something from the latest series and she'll wander off after five minutes, but we watched the whole of *The Web Planet* episode one without her getting bored. So that's a start. I'm an evangelist. I'm always trying to convert people. I'm like a Scientologist for Doctor Who.

Ben Lawrence

TV and radio commissioning editor at the Telegraph
Inadvertently announced the embargoed title of
The Waters of Mars *in an issue of Total TV Guide*

It is hard to believe now, but there was a hint of cynicism in the air in March 2005. Us lifelong Doctor Who fans had been dreaming of a regeneration for nearly 16 years, but of course we had been here before. In 1996, Paul McGann and The TV Movie had tried to breathe life into a dead franchise, but had twisted the premise into a cod US imagining of what a British science fiction show might be. It was unexciting and, crucially, lacking in any charm.

"It was the moment that Doctor Who was elevated from tea-time whimsy."

The press launch for Russell T Davies's new series in Cardiff proved that the BBC had faith in it. They had invited celebrities (Charlotte Church, Robson Green, Matt Lucas), produced proper canapes and, unfortunately for me, not stinted on the wine.

And then the screening. I can still feel the whizz of adrenaline. *Rose* lasted 45 minutes but it seemed to last seconds. A tightly constructed story, its use of Autons was inspired, their aesthetic blending in perfectly to 21st century TV. It was funny. And Billie Piper as Rose silenced all the naysayers with her touching, heartfelt performance.

But it was a speech that really struck me. Christopher Eccleston's "Now forget me, Rose Tyler" was unlike anything the series had witnessed before. It was the Doctor as Prospero and the moment that Doctor Who was elevated from tea-time whimsy to award-winning drama. Enjoyable, always. But now with something genuinely important to say. I was grinning from ear to ear.

As was everyone after the launch. Barry Letts was there, looking exactly as he did in 1973. This wise old guardian of the show clearly approved. As did Terrance Dicks, although you could tell that razor-sharp mind had been unpicking the structure and the dialogue, wondering what he would have done better.

And that was it. The day Doctor Who became a critic's choice, the day the world changed. The day I drank too much red wine and got black lips, and had to later endure an army of Autons marching through my head. Still, it was all worth it.

Martina Cole

Author
Always wanted to use the TARDIS to go back in time and see Jimi Hendrix play

I've got to be honest with you, I actually prefer the original Doctor. William Hartnell was fantastic, he always reminded me of Catweazle, with that mad hair and everything.

"I think red Daleks are mummy Daleks."

But what really frightened me was when Barbara and Ian walked into that police box for the first time and it was just so huge and futuristic inside. I was only three, but I'd never seen anything like it in my little life. I used to watch it with my older sister, who was six years older than me, on my mum and dad's old horsehair settee.

Then, of course, came the first appearance of the Daleks, which was from the point of view of a Dalek itself. My friend's mother said, "Oh don't be silly, it's a plunger from the bathroom." I was terrified, going, "No, no it's not!" I was really frightened of it.

It kicked off a fascination with sci-fi and the supernatural which I've had all my life. I'm obsessed with the stars, outer space and things like that. I'd love to go up in a rocket, I really would.

The house I live in is haunted. The first night we moved in, I slept in the same room as my daughter because it's a big property and I thought she might be a bit scared. In the middle of the night I was woken by an awful noise and this rasping voice. I looked up and there was this green eye staring from the corner of the room. Well, I jumped out of the bed in fright.

Then I heard what it was saying. "You are an enemy of the Daleks!" It was her Doctor Who alarm clock. I thought we were having a visitation. She slept right through it.

Our house has now turned into a Doctor Who zone. I think we've pretty much got every DVD they've released. When my daughter was three and a half — she's a teenager now — she would watch Doctor Who sitting on my lap. I'll never forget what she said to me: "I think the red Dalek is the mummy Dalek." I remember wondering, "Well, what does that make me?" I think it's because they were ordering everyone around. Because that's what mummies do. They're in charge. It really cracked me up.

Richard Dinnick

Author and journalist
Wrote The Big Finish Companion, a complete guide to the official Doctor Who audio adventures

I never knew my father. There is no particular mystery to this, he just chose not to be a part of my life. As a youngster, growing up in the depths of Surrey, male role models were pretty thin on the ground. I did have my older brother. While he didn't exactly measure up as a father figure, what he did do was get me watching Doctor Who.

Watching Doctor Who every Saturday was a family ritual, from before I was born. My first memory of anything on telly was Doctor Who. I must have become aware of it properly during *Day of the Daleks*, aged three, because, although my first real memory is watching a Dalek appear in disused railway tunnel, I thought the Controller was the Master. Well, they seemed to share a tailor…

"My mum told me yes, I was half Time Lord."

I was totally freaked out by that Dalek. It was the first time I'd ever seen one! But it was okay. The Doctor was there. With no father to latch onto, my three-year-old self fixed on Jon Pertwee's charming, dashing, heroic portrayal like a laser-guided imprint device. To me, the Third Doctor wasn't just "my Doctor". He was my dad!

I guess therapy should have been the logical route but my mum encouraged this fantasy, telling me yes, I was half Time Lord! And with him off fighting Daleks and Drashigs every week, it certainly explained my absentee parent.

But the Doctor also helped shape my moral compass. When I grew up, I wanted to be like him. I hope that I would have made him proud and that when I write stories for him, I get him right. It's the least I can do.

James Goss

Writer, former BBC Doctor Who web site producer
Accidentally pitched a TV series named S-Club Blake's 7 in an attempt to get out of an ideas development meeting

When I was a kid, I'd always wanted to know what it was like to be a Doctor Who monster. The answer is smelly, and painful. I'd been off work with the summer cold (everyone was claiming to have "caught it off David", natch) when the phone call came through: "We need a Cyberman tomorrow."

"I'm ill," I croaked. "I'm running a fever!"

"We'll be meeting at the hotel. It's got air-conditioning. It'll be fun. It'll take your mind off it."

So I turned up at the hotel.

Dressing up as a Cyberman is enormous fun. I recommend it. It takes about half an hour, and it feels like being embalmed in someone else's old socks. The costume itself reeked and the neckpiece was like a giant rubber throat corset. I imagined I was being gently throttled by invisible hands. I couldn't walk, I couldn't breathe, but at least the air-conditioning was blissful.

An hour later, I was standing in a park, in the middle of one of Cardiff's rare heatwaves. The traditional cure for a cold is to lie down with comfort food and a boxset, not bake yourself in foam rubber. Still, the nice thing about the neckpiece was that I'd stopped coughing.

"I have never, ever wanted to be sick more."

We were filming a DVD extra about what monsters do on their day off. Paul Kasey, the main Cyberman actor, and I started to play a game of football. Paul wore the suit as though it was made for him (actually, it was). He tackled me effortlessly, slammed home goal after goal and then did the Peter Crouch robot dance. I tottered and wheezed a little.

Paul suggested we go on the roundabout. Seen through the peep-holes in the helmet, it was a horrible sensation.

"Scream if you want to go faster!" yelled Paul. I shut my eyes. It made things worse.

Disoriented by the helmet and the spinning, I couldn't work out what I was seeing. It was like the space-time tunnel in 2001, but with an adventure playground. I staggered off the roundabout making the pre-arranged "Help!" signal.

The helmet came off. I have never, ever wanted to be sick more. I leaned over. I heaved. And nothing came out. It was the rubber neck band, so tight I couldn't possibly throw up. I just stood there, green and hiccuping.

I noticed Paul Kasey, still fully suited. Somehow, the normally impassive Cyberface appeared to be smirking.

Paul J Salamoff

Comic book author, Hollywood make-up effects guru
Bumped into Sergeant Benton at his local photocopy and print shop in California

I am cursed by being American. Doctor Who wasn't easy to come by growing up in the early 1970s but, as luck would have it, I lived near Boston, Massachusetts, the home of Channel 2 aka WGBH. It was a public broadcasting network run by donor (i.e. viewer) support. As a consequence, they were also the only station on TV to show Doctor Who.

My first memory of the show came many years before I realised it was even Doctor Who. A black and white image burned itself into my young brain of a woman being terrorised in a barn by a humanoid reptilian monstrosity. It haunted me for many years.

As a teenager, I stumbled upon a quirky sci-fi show from the UK about a man who travels in time and space in a blue box that was bigger on the inside. WGBH showed the complete 12th season, which I watched religiously, then started it again from the beginning (I happily re-watched the entire season). Second time round, after *Revenge of the Cybermen*, they moved on to *Terror of the Zygons* and the rest of season 13.Then on and on until Peter Davison became the Doctor. I was addicted.

Then something magical happened — WGBH mixed things up and started to show Jon Pertwee stories. His second adventure was *Doctor Who and the Silurians*. At the time, it only existed in black and white and, as episode two was working up to its cliffhanger, the Doctor's friend Liz Shaw ran into a barn and was attacked by a humanoid reptilian monstrosity.

> **"As a teenager, I stumbled upon a quirky sci-fi show."**

There it was! The nightmare image that had terrified me for so many years and it was from Doctor Who. Even though I was much older by then and not prone to being scared so much, the frightened five-year-old boy in me wanted to run and hide behind the sofa.

Lindsay Duncan

Actress

Played Captain Adelaide Brooke in The Waters of Mars

My Doctor Who story, I am often told, is really a very disturbing, dark and emotional episode. Personally, I haven't actually got a context to put it in. I don't know if it was darker than any of the others, for example. Were the monsters more frightening? I'm not in a position to say. Again, with the moral ambiguity of the Doctor, I don't know if it's been broached before. It's really interesting. Is it something that the adults pick up on but is lost on the kids?

Children have always — historically, through fairytales at the very least — met darkness. And they have to really. Whatever the modern equivalent is, kids psychologically need to address it from a safe place. Russell T Davies is a real force for good in television, and that really attracted me. He really understands where Doctor Who sits with the audience. He's someone who likes to explore, who finds the fun of the adventure. Any writer who is worth their salt will seize the chance of the almost limitless possibilities that Doctor Who offers.

So what made me want to do it was Russell, really. Although I wouldn't necessarily have wanted to play a monster.

Thankfully, my character didn't turn into one of the zombie creatures, so it was vital that I didn't get at all wet. But there were other sacrifices. I can't remember what time of year it was but it was really cold. The two guys who were the first to go down, they were wretched. Miserable. They had contact lenses in and were soaking all the time.

David Tennant, of course, was amazing. Fast in every way: a fast brain, a fast talker, and fast on his feet. And, because I'm slightly older than him, I felt really competitive about the running. I ran as fast as I could to keep up but, because I didn't warm up properly, I pulled a muscle — I suppose it was punishment for my vanity — and that lived with me for a little while after we finished. Clearly I must give up running. It doesn't work. Serves me right for wanting to be a show-off.

That said, it's important, with a long-running show like this, that the people who work on it full-time get an opportunity to show off *their* skills — and they really do on Doctor Who. It was an impressive production. It keeps the enthusiasm going when you're working that hard. You really believe you are in this strange but beautiful alien landscape.

"You really believe you are in this strange but beautiful alien landscape."

If I have one regret, though, it's that I'll now never work with the Eleventh Doctor. Matt Smith and I are great friends and, when he got Doctor Who, I was thrilled for him. I'm really taken with the new era as well, I think it's fantastic — although, to be honest, I watched a few just because of Matt. But it's very sad because it's apparently illegal to bring back Adelaide. It's not going to happen. It's a shame because it would've been great fun.

Mat Irvine

Doctor Who visual effects designer and K-9's "caretaker"
Changed the metal mutt's name plate to read "K-Y" for a Lily Savage sketch in 1997

Every time we went into studios to film Doctor Who, we'd always take in a pile of spare props because we knew they'd be wanted for use in the background, scattered about the set. It was usually the sort of things the story's prop buyer or the set designer hadn't thought of: stuff that would get pointed at in the distance. Actually, as we were filming The Hitchhikers Guide to the Galaxy and Blake's 7 at roughly the same time, if you were sharp-eyed you could probably see the same props appearing in all three series.

For *Warriors of the Deep* — not my favourite episode but there we are — at the very beginning of episode one, the set was an undersea base. As per, we had all these futuristic bits and bobs with us, and started sticking them in the background. The director walked right over, picked up one of our knackered props, and put it bang in front of camera: "Okay, Big Close Up, folks. We're going to start…"

Of course, the thing was rubbish. So it was literally was a panic to get it to look at least half-way reasonable in time for the guy to shout "Action!". I'm not talking HD-ready but we had to tart up this piece of something-or-other so that it could withstand its BCU for the beginning of this particular episode. But we did it. That's what we were there for. To think on our feet.

Believe it or not, we — the BBC Visual Effects Department — used to have to phone up the Doctor Who Appreciation Society to ask them, "Which way does the TARDIS revolve?" because we had to film it every few weeks for each new director who came on board. Every new Doctor Who story was treated, as far as the bean counters were concerned, as an individual programme. This is before the days when we had stock shots. We'd say, "It's a waste of film, y'know, we've got this thing in the can already," but the directors would always insist on new footage for their episodes... "Er, does the light flash when it's materialising or not?"

"Which way does the TARDIS revolve?"

And, basically, the answer was... nobody quite knew: "If it's from the top, it's anti-clockwise, with the light flashing. Or is it anti-clockwise if it's going backwards in time, but clockwise if it's going forward in time...?" For an entire generation, there was no established way for the TARDIS to fly through space. No wonder the Doctor had so much trouble with it!

Polly Adams
Daughter of Douglas
Was once sent a large collection of Doctor Who stamps, completely anonymously — an incident that has never been explained

So I spent a long time trying to pin down my single favourite thing about Doctor Who, and I was getting absolutely nowhere.

Was it the people? The running down corridors? The wibbly-wobbly timey-wimey?

It wasn't until I saw the lifesize Karen Gillan cardboard cut-out standing next to my desk that it hit me.

(This thought, not the cutout. Although that has happened too.)

What's particularly brilliant about Doctor Who is not that it's a long-standing 45-minute television show on a Saturday night. There are a lot of those. The particular brilliance of Doctor Who is that it is so much *more* than that. It's such an integral part of my life, and the lives of so many others, in the way that television rarely achieves. That's what I love the most about Doctor Who.

A great example of that, for me, is this: I remember standing out the back of the Sydney Opera House during the interval of the Doctor Who Symphonic Spectacular, surrounded by girls dressed as Daleks and looking through the great glass walls that overlook the harbour. I remember thinking to myself that of all the sunsets I've seen in my life, that was the most special. And I wouldn't have been there, sharing in something spectacular, if it weren't for the Doctor.

"It's such an integral part of my life."

But, beyond all that, the 45 minutes on a Saturday evening is pretty great too.

Perhaps the most meaningful expression of my love for Doctor Who, though, is simply that the day I found out my award-winning, best-selling author of a father wrote for Doctor Who was the day I was most proud to call myself his daughter.

Scott Lynch

Author and volunteer firefighter
Formally announced the disposal of his collection of off-air VHS Doctor Who recordings in a tweet dated March 22nd 2012

I first experienced a sort of parallel-universe version of Doctor Who, in that I came to it entirely through a set of creased and dog-eared paperback novelisations at the local library. From these, and from a few Peter Haining reference books I dug out of the hoary cellars of the Dewey Decimal 700s, I constructed an elaborate and wildly erroneous mental impression of what Doctor Who must look and sound like. This private sensory vocabulary of the series naturally crumbled the instant it made contact with the genuine article!

It was 1989. I was 11, and American, and I had absolutely no idea that the show I was falling in love with by proxy in my own imagination was almost at that very minute being cancelled by a BBC that had grown strangely tired of having a lucrative international success on its hands. I can only imagine that someone thought a licence to print money was a very tedious thing to have cluttering up the place.

"A licence to print money was a very tedious thing to have cluttering up the place."

Anyhow, I didn't get to properly glimpse televised Doctor Who until the autumn of 1990, when my local PBS affiliate began one of its periodic re-runs, commencing with Tom Baker's debut serial *Robot* (known to me from paperback as Doctor Who and the Giant Robot). I was thoroughly bewildered by the look of the videography and the devolution of scale; what had been an epic battle with a cast of thousands in my head had somehow turned into half-a-dozen people flopping about in dark corridors while a CSO robot menaced toy trucks. All set to the music of what I presumed was a single creepy and disgruntled bassoonist!

How bewilderment rapidly became love, I don't quite know. Perhaps it was that genuine Doctor Who was as singular and strange as my imaginary Doctor Who. It looked and sounded like nothing on American television and the rest of my family found it (like my enthusiasm for it) incomprehensible, so they generously left the television entirely at my disposal for that glorious mid-Sunday hour when PBS would unroll two more episodes. I was left alone to appreciate it, and so even as Who ceased to be a private mental vision for me it remained a private experience, a sort of meditative nerd idyll in which I could ponder the show free of judgment or distraction. I soon found myself paging through my astronomy books as I watched, imagining a TARDIS behind every wispy nebula and hurtling across every galactic disk.

Nothing that has happened to the show since, or ever will happen to it, can steal my memories of a time when grainy video and pop-gun special effects would routinely transmute to glorious cosmic vistas behind my eyes. I'd be lying if I said it didn't still happen from time to time. How can you ever get over something as magical as that? Why would you want to?

Sean Williams

Author

Published an atheist dissection of the series entitled Doctor Who and the Legacy of Rationalism

My relationship with Doctor Who is utterly conventional, from hiding as a child behind the couch during *Revenge of the Cybermen* to developing an obsession that extended as far as the novelisations, which I inhaled at an enormous rate and still have today, preserved next to my brag shelf (an array of books and magazines that my own work has appeared in). Battered and tattered by multiple readings though they are, their value is incalculable, to me.

I like to say, somewhat flippantly, that Pertwee's Doctor made me an atheist and Terrance Dicks made me a writer. Just how true the latter is came home to me the year I turned 40. Not only was I getting married for the first time, but I was also buying my first home and launching the first book in a new series, the first with a new publisher. But what was I most stressed about? A short story called Midnight at the Cafe of the Black Madonna, published in Destination Prague, one of Big Finish's anthologies edited by Steven Savile. It was an official Third Doctor story, approved by the Beeb and everything, and I had written it.

> **"Pertwee's Doctor made me an atheist and Terrance Dicks made me a writer."**

The canonical status of such stories will always be in question, but that didn't matter to me, not one jot. This was my chance to tell a story I'd always wanted to tell (what happened to the Doctor between Jo Grant and Sarah Jane Smith) and an opportunity to bring my career full circle, back to the source, as it were. Doctor Who really did make me who I am in several critical ways. I wasn't giving back so much as tying the bow.

Only as publication neared did it occur to me that, while on one level this was just a story, a tie-in like several others I had written, on another it was a huge symbolic risk. If I failed at this task, if I didn't capture Pertwee's voice or the concerns of his time — or above all write a fun and interesting Doctor Who adventure — what would that mean? I imagined a single, deafening pop followed by the painfully elongated deflation of my career, accompanied by a rude-sounding raspberry.

Many writers have survived this crisis, with much more at stake than me. I survived along with them. The point is not the story itself but the act of transubstantiation it underwent in my mind, from nostalgic exercise to full-blown creative litmus test. How does a kids' show from 50 years ago manage such a profound effect on someone who is both an adult and a professional writer?

By being consistently worth the investment I made as a child, and continue to make now. That's what I think, anyway. Whether it's true or not, today's children can make up their own minds, 50 years hence.

Simon Furman

Comic book writer
Contributed three comic strip stories to Doctor Who Magazine in the 1980s, including one entitled A Cold Day In Hell

As with so much TV in the 1960s and 1970s, watching was a whole family pastime, hardly ever a solo or kids' thing (especially at weekends). I always used to slightly resent my parents intruding on what felt like "our" programmes. But it toughened you up. If you showed you were scared, which I often was, you were likely to find yourself banished. My abiding childhood memory is of *The Ice Warriors*, back in the Troughton era, and stomping around our back garden in cricket pads pretending to be one.

I've experienced almost the entire length and breadth of Doctor Who, as a viewer first and foremost, but I was also a big reader. I loved the paperback novels and adaptations. It felt like you got so much extra stuff in those — detail that you missed in the episodes, or extra levels of character. In many ways, the Target novels pushed me into writing as much as my love of comics. As a kid, I think I got the best of the series, when it was still truly terrifying (simply because we were so under-exposed to that kind of stuff, unlike today) and, as an adult, I can sit back and appreciate the skill and dexterity of the current writers and actors.

The big lesson I think I learned was: never write down to your audience — and, even while (back in the day) it was firmly aimed at kids, Doctor Who never did. It hit you with monsters and mad science and matters of life and death. That, I believe, is the reason for its enduring success. And it's something I've always tried to apply to my own writing.

I once worked in an office with a big Doctor Who fan. He knew who I was (and, yes, he *was* impressed) mostly because of my Who writing credentials. I milked that for all it was worth. The downside was I felt I had to temper my own geekiness, in case it ruined my "professional" demeanour. I used to scorn some of his gushing excesses. Oh, how two-faced!

"I got the best of the series, when it was still truly terrifying."

I had plenty of script work at the time but the idea of eventually writing an Ice Warriors comic strip was just obsessional. So I badgered and cajoled the Doctor Who Magazine team until I got a shot. And was then told that there were problems with using the Ice Warriors (some kind of ownership issue that required a royalty payment). I was gutted. So I put my second love, werewolves, into that particular story. But I got to do my Ice Warriors tale in the end.

And I still do the cricket pad thing, incidentally.

Stephen Baxter
Author
Wrote The Wheel of Ice, both a prequel and sequel to The Wheel in Space (but that's time travel for you)

As a kid I always loved Doctor-Who-in-space stories, such as *The Wheel in Space*, the 1968 serial which introduced super-brainy astrophysicist companion Zoe working on the eponymous deep-space station. And because co-writer Kit Pedler, a bona fide scientist, was an unofficial science advisor for the series, serials like this made pleasing technical sense. Well, to some extent.

But where exactly was the Wheel? You might think we know that very precisely from this dialogue:

> BILL DUGGAN: I just like flowers. Hey… That one comes all the way from Venus. Imagine that. All those millions of miles away.
> ZOE: 24,564,000 miles at perihelion and 161,350,000 miles at aphelion.
> JAMIE: Oh, I was dying to know that…

Wow! Boffin terms and precise numbers. So that's where the Wheel is… but what does Zoe mean?

Perhaps the Wheel follows an elliptical, oval-shaped, orbit around the sun – like a comet's orbit rather than a planet's circular orbit. "Perihelion" means an orbiting object's closest approach to the sun; "aphelion" means the furthest distance. If Zoe's numbers refer to the station's orbit, the Wheel would travel from inside Mercury's orbit to outside Mars's, a useful patrol for a deep-space station.

But Zoe mentioned Venus. And that's more puzzling; how close the station gets to Venus at aphelion would depend on where Venus is in its own orbit at the time. So what do the numbers mean?

"Serials like this made a pleasing technical sense… to some extent."

You can spin lots of theories, but consider this. Earth's orbit is 93 million miles in radius; Venus's is 68 million miles. So the closest Earth gets to Venus, when the two planets are on the same side of the sun, is (93-68=) 25 million miles. Similarly the furthest Earth gets from Venus is (93+68=) 161 million miles. And these two numbers are precisely those Zoe quotes. So her statement would make sense if the Wheel is in Earth orbit! But then the Wheel wouldn't be much use as a deep-space station…

Science advisor or not, that bit of dialogue is just gobbledegook after all. Never mind! This was a good serial, and Zoe was one of my favourite companions. But we don't know where her Wheel in Space is, and never will.

Konnie Huq

TV presenter
Dressed up in Tom Baker's costume for a celebratory episode of Blue Peter

I knew all about the Cybermen long before I saw them on television. Such is the power of Doctor Who; it seeps into your consciousness. The books and magazines people brought into school had all the information necessary to fuel my nightmares.

Cybermen could paralyse you. They had a single aim, to make you like them: giant, cyborg, plastic creatures devoid of personality or emotion. And they owned Cybermat pets who would poison your blood and make your veins throb red. But more than that, it was their eyes. Blank, soulless, hollow circles with nothing inside. That was what really put the fear into me.

It was only later, when I finally saw them in an episode that I realised they had a weakness: gold. After that, I didn't feel quite so scared. If they could be beaten, then I could almost feel sorry for them. When they chased you, arms outstretched, perhaps they were actually reaching for something they'd lost, their humanity.

I always thought it'd be awesome to play the Doctor's assistant. Who knows, though, maybe one day they'll even have a female Doctor. That'd be interesting...

However, my strongest memory of Doctor Who is a slightly embarrassing one. I interviewed Christopher Eccleston and he dropped lots of hints that he wasn't coming back after his first series. I wished him luck for the following year and he said, "We'll see." So, arguably, I missed a scoop on that one. But then, much later on, at a party, I walked up to David Tennant and asked him, "Hey, why didn't you just tell me you were leaving?" I was a bit tired and delirious, so I think I'd started to believe that all the Doctors were the same person (in real life as well as on the television). But that's the persuasive power of Doctor Who.

> **"Maybe one day they'll even have a female Doctor."**

Hugh Bonneville

Actor

As a child, lived for a time in the same street in Blackheath, South East London, as Sophie Aldred

I have vivid memories of going round to my grandmother's house on a Saturday afternoon to watch Final Score and then take up my position behind the sofa in time for the opening titles of Doctor Who. As with lots of kids of my generation, it was the highlight of the weekend. Yet for some reason my memory is also tinged with melancholy.

Maybe it was the desultory cadence in the voice of the guy who read out the football results — "Dundee United 2, Motherwell 0" — it was so depressing; or maybe it had something to do with my grandmother's furniture: a forbidding, rather itchy, bottle green three-piece suite. Grandma poured the tea then vacated the room, to go and do whatever grandmas do on a Saturday afternoon, confident that for the duration of Doctor Who, at least, I would be transfixed.

> **"I still get a chill thinking about Cybermen emerging from manholes."**

Once the titles and music started, it meant that I was going to be, if not frightened, at least stirred in some uncomfortable way. I remember being very concerned about Brigadier Lethbridge-Stewart, running around various chalk pits. Also, because I knew London a bit, I was terrified to see the Cybermen coming out of manholes and plodding about under the railway arches in what I took to be Southwark, near Guy's Hospital. There's a particular road near London Bridge station which chills me whenever I drive along it even today, just remembering that episode. For all I know the sequence was filmed miles away but it's lodged in my imagination as that street and that's what counts.

Wind forward 35 years or so and, as a childhood fan, if not an adult aficionado, I kept asking my agent to badger the casting director, Andy Pryor, about finding me a part. Eventually he said, "Shut up! We'll let you know when we find something suitable."

Some time later, after I'd finished filming the first series of Downton Abbey and Twenty Twelve back-to-back I slumped into a heap and wallowed in the prospect of not having to shave at 5am every day. The resulting beard became quite piratical in its bushiness and I guess Andy or one of the producers saw a photo and thought, "Well, we've got a pirate episode coming up... he'll do!"

When my agent sent me the script of *The Curse of the Black Spot*, I looked at page one, phoned her up and said, "I'm in." I wasn't expecting it to be such a cracking part and such a brilliantly written episode. Plus, there's something quite reassuring about pirates. You know where you are with them. Or at least you think you do.

But nothing's quite as it seems in Doctor Who, and I rather like that this crew turn out to be terrified victims rather than marauding buccaneers. And I love the final image of them sailing off on their new ship... into space.

It was a great stand-alone story: funny, adventurous, with serious tension and a great twist. Stephen Thompson did a great job. It had its own flavour while being part of the continuing story. That's what's so wonderful about this show, that each episode has a completely blank canvas. The boundaries of the storylines are those of the writers' imaginations.

I've heard a fan theory that the pirates in this episode somehow become the antagonists of Patrick Troughton's penultimate story, *The Space Pirates*. All I can say is, I'm up for that.

A spin-off series? Bring it on.

Iain Morris

Writer, producer, co-creator of The Inbetweeners
Went to university with Christian Hinchcliffe, son of seminal Doctor Who producer Phillip Hinchcliffe

I'd heard a lot of people talking — older boys, mainly — about how awesome Doctor Who was, but I'd never seen it. I'd been told, I honestly had been told, that it was so scary you had to watch from behind the sofa.

So, when the new series finally arrived — and after checking with my mum that it was suitable for me — I did.

What with the radiator and the window sill, there wasn't much room back there, but it wasn't long before I had clambered over and was sitting watching, rapt. I loved the Doctor. In his cricket whites and hat, I genuinely thought he looked the epitome of cool. And for the next three years I watched religiously, never scared, but always amazed by just how cool Peter Davison was as the Doctor.

"I didn't think you could 'have' two Doctors."

Now I'm aware that this isn't a popular opinion. In fact, just now, my colleague Damon has read what I'm writing over my shoulder and said, "Peter Davison was rubbish," but he's wrong and he smells, and is a bad driver and has terrible taste in clothes.

He's stopped reading now, so I'll go back to my point which is that, in fact, Peter Davison was the most stylish, believable and interesting Doctor ever.

And I'm not intending to cite any examples or "proof" (proof is for evolutionists) as to why he was the best Doctor. But he was younger and better looking than Tom Baker, and just effortlessly cool.

Who else could pull off a boater, a white blazer and a leek brooch? He was a perfect amalgamation of what I still think are the coolest things ever — cricket and aliens.

Obviously Baker and McCoy had an impossible act to follow, as did McGann and it was only after the Gallifreyan soil had lain fallow — yes, I know, it's a figure of speech — could anyone come along to challenge my concrete opinion: David Tennant.

I didn't think you could "have" two Doctors. I thought that you had one and he was yours, like a football team, but then David Tennant was just too good to ignore.

(Although, Matt Smith is a bit brilliant, isn't he? Like he was born to do it.)

Steve Cole

Writer

Learned the planet he invented for a novel was actually pronounced 'Jus-TISH-ee-A', not 'Jus-TISS-ee-a', when Rose mentioned it in Boom Town.

I was six years old. In a bookshop. Doctor Who and the Revenge of the Cybermen was clutched in my hands. My mother, wary of forking out 40p on a child's whim, made me read the first page aloud to be sure it wasn't beyond me.

There was a lot riding on my performance but I pulled it off, merrily making up the words I couldn't read (it was science-fiction, which to my mum is pretty much a foreign language anyway). I needed that book – back in the 1970s, barring the odd repeat, the only way to re-acquaint yourself with the Doctor's past adventures was by reading.

"My mother made me read the first page aloud."

And boy, did I ever read.

In some ways, the books became more important to me than the TV show. There were scores to collect, and they offered a kind of comforting permanence, shoring up the uncertainties of childhood. Depending on which body he wore, the Doctor might have "a shock of white hair" or "a tangle of unruly curls", or a "pleasant, open face" " but he always had "capacious pockets" and a ship that arrived with a "wheezing, groaning sound". This familiarity lent young readers confidence as they worked their way through the Doctor's literary universe — and gave young writers a heap of ways to impress their English teachers.

Former Who script-editor Terrance Dicks wrote most of these books (the novelisation of *Revenge of the Cybermen* included), translating screen-fare into prose with verve and economy. Terrance gave a talk at my local library in 1980. I was there in the front row.

That talk crystallised something in me; aged nine, I knew I wanted to be a writer, like him. It was an ambition that eventually came true, but before that our paths were to cross again…

Doctor Who in print was a relentless beast and in 1997 I found myself at BBC Worldwide, editing the ongoing series of books featuring the Eighth Doctor and his various past selves.

The first author I worked with?

Terrance Dicks. The man who'd helped me learn to read and inspired me to write. Through a trick of time and space there we were again, and we've remained on friendly terms to this day — with the ageless Doctor still at our backs.

 ## Paul McAuley

Author
Wrote a 40th anniversary celebratory Doctor Who novella, The Eye of the Tyger

It was the day after the assassination of President Kennedy, Saturday, 23 November 1963. I knew, because my mother told me, because it was all over the radio and TV, that JFK's death was both terrible and terribly important, but I didn't know why. I was only eight, after all. I was far more interested in the new BBC children's programme, billed in the Radio Times as "an adventure in time and space".

I was already a stone cold science-fiction fan. I loved the novels of Jules Verne and Patrick Moore (H. G. Wells came a little later) and read everything like them I could find – even Captain W. E. Johns' terrible Lucius Brane novels. So at 5.15pm that Saturday I was front and centre as the TV set clanged and throbbed with eerie electronic music and a rushing kaleidoscope pattern (in state-of-the art 405-line black and white) that slowly faded to a foggy night and a perfectly ordinary policeman pacing past a perfectly ordinary scrapyard. The camera turned away from him to show a police box tucked away in a corner... the beginning of the mystery on which that first episode turned: who was the Doctor?

Most of the story was about two young teachers, Ian and Barbara, and their concern for one of their pupils, Susan Foreman, a bright but otherwordly girl who was bullied by the other children. Although Susan's modern comprehensive was quite unlike the small rural Church of England primary school I attended (and I wasn't especially bullied), like many bright, oddball kids I instantly identified with her.

Ian and Barbara decide to pay a home visit, and are confronted in the scrapyard by Susan's grandfather, "A crotchety old man at least 745 years old," as the show's creator, Sydney Newman, observed. For me, just a child, this fearsome apparition, with his haughty, impatient manner, Edwardian costume and white mane brushed back from a severe face, was as terrifying as any monster. Somehow, the two adults push past him and enter the police box, and find it is bigger on the inside: a bright, futuristic space. And the Doctor whirls his machine and passengers into the deep past, and we were off on a wild jaunt that 50 years later isn't yet over.

> ## "A haughty, impatient manner, Edwardian costume and white mane."

I remember it so clearly not because of its proximity to the trauma of Kennedy's assassination but because it was repeated the next week, just before the second episode — the BBC thought that its audience might have been too stunned to take it in. And because it was the beginning of a TV series that seemed to have been made just for me: that fitted, exactly, a space in my head I hadn't realised was there, until those first utterly enthralling 25 minutes.

Bonnie Langford

Actress, played the Doctor's companion Mel
Performed her first press call with Colin Baker on a Kirby wire dressed as Peter Pan

I don't know if I have a favourite memory of Doctor Who but I have some strange ones. Usually my first thoughts are either of peculiar monsters and creatures with weird costumes or being cold and wet in quarries on location.

One of the things that I know was very representative of Doctor Who when I was in it were all the guest stars. We had quite an eclectic and glittering mix. People like Geoffrey Hughes, Honor Blackman, Kate O'Mara, Ken Dodd, and Stubby Kaye — I thought he was incredible: to me he was Mr Musical Theatre, yet there he was in Wales being in Doctor Who. It was a Who's Who of showbiz luvvies for a while.

We had one scene in *Time and the Rani* with Wanda Ventham and killer bees. It was all CGI'd afterwards, but someone had to do a dying scene after being stung by one of these bees. I think the take they used in the finished episode was the only one that didn't have someone cracking up on it. Whether it was good, bad or indifferent, they had to put it in because there wasn't another clean take.

We once did a whole sequence of stuff with Sylvester McCoy on a motorbike. Literally every single time he got on the bike, though, it would stall. One time he almost drove over a cliff. We had so many out-takes they made it into a VT and played Leader of the Pack over it at the wrap party.

Although I didn't do any singing in the show, the producer did ask me to scream in the key of E for the end of one particular episode. It was, effectively, the final note before the theme tune crashed in underneath, so the idea was it would blend in. Then it became a running gag. I'd take the mick and ask them what key they wanted: "Now scream in the key of F sharp." Then they asked me to scream a little quieter because I was distorting the cameras.

> **"For the end of one episode, the producer asked me to scream in the key of E."**

I played Mel for two seasons of Doctor Who and I enjoyed it for a while, but it was time to move on. The character was quite one dimensional and, although I was very earnest in my commitment to find depth and meaning, I'm not sure it was there to be found! Now the assistants have a more fully written and helpful purpose in their efforts to accompany and support the Doctor in his adventures.

My leaving scene wasn't very exciting — if anything a little too sentimental — but at least I wasn't killed off. I just went to a super-market in the sky. I'm probably still trying to find my way out. Stuck at the checkout in a space ASDA.

Mike Carey

Graphic novelist
Once pulled the main lever on the TARDIS, but couldn't make it go VWORP VWORP (ergo, not a Time Lord)

I started watching Doctor Who when I was about five — way too young to understand what was going on, most of the time, but old enough to be drawn in by the weirdness and scariness and general excitement.

"A fat boy with bad eyesight, wearing full school uniform."

I was a sensitive soul, and the show was too much for me on a regular basis. Strangely though, the thing that scared me the most wasn't conventionally frightening at all. It was a moment in *The Celestial Toymaker*. The Toymaker himself, played by Michael Gough, is trying to best the Doctor and his assistants in a series of rigged games. If they lose, they will be turned into toys and added to the Toymaker's collection. Bwa-ha-ha.

But they keep winning, against the odds, and finally the Toymaker gets a monologue where he says he's going to bring his biggest gun into play — the deadliest item in his armoury, the ultimate weapon. "The Doctor won't stand the ghost of a snowman's cat in hell's chance against this!" he gloats. (I paraphrase, but only a little.)

He looks off into the wings, arms raised to summon this terrifying entity. And in it comes.

And it's Billy Bunter, the beloved comic hero of Frank Richards' boarding school stories — a fat boy with bad eyesight, wearing full school uniform.

My head just about exploded at this point. I couldn't process the gap between the Toymaker's words and this banal, reassuring reality. This was the worst monster of all? What in the name of God was it going to do?

And I don't think I ever actually found out. I missed the next episode, which was the last in the serial, and it's never been collected on video or DVD. In fact, I think the episodes are among those that are currently missing in action.

So this incongruous figure still pops up in my nightmares from time to time, and I always wake up whimpering. But I think that's the magic of Doctor Who, in a nutshell. It messes with all of our heads, but each of us gets to be traumatised in a unique and special way.

Michael Kibble-White

Retired management consultant
Niece worked on a pilot for a sci-fi show with Jon Pertwee — but it didn't take off

I watched Doctor Who from the very first episode in 1963. How did it begin?

I was 24, and newly married. We were living in Crawley in Sussex and I worked as an engineer at Mullard Ltd, who manufactured electrical components. At the weekends we went dinghy sailing at a club in Felpham, close to Bognor Regis.

There was a very scatty, well-spoken professor-type called John Sharp, who ran it. At the end of the day, he'd always invite us back to his home, White Lodge. It sounded very posh, but the house was a shambles. Someone once said to him, "John, don't you ever decorate this place?" He replied, "Frequently — with my presence."

"It was weird and unlike anything else on television."

We'd eat bacon rind sandwiches, because he could get them cheap from the butcher, and we'd watch TV. It was at White Lodge I saw the very first episode of Doctor Who. It grabbed me — you didn't know what was going to happen, didn't know where it was going. You came back next week, and you were constantly surprised by it. It was weird and unlike anything else on television.

We didn't stop watching. When I became a father, I watched it with my kids. They have fond memories of Saturday nights in the 1970s with Tom Baker on the TV, and us playing the card game, Happy Families.

"A man is a sum of his memories" — I'm told that's something the Doctor once said. It's a bit sweeping, isn't it? But it's true. Having given it some 10 seconds of thought, it's true!

I'm not aware of my memory deteriorating — until I get the feeling I ought to know something; I think about it, and I can't remember. It's very frustrating. I was diagnosed with Alzheimer's in 2008. It seems like such a long time ago now. What did I think when the doctor told me? I can't tell you. I can't recall. It's a horrible condition.

Am I scared? No. I think I'm still in control. And I think this book is a good thing.

Acknowledgments

Many thanks to all those friends, acquaintances, agents and celebrities who helped to compile this collection of memories about the world's best TV series. There are far too many to name individually but particular mention must be made of Neil Sloan, Lisa Lambert, Peter Thomas, Carolyn Djanogly, and Lorraine Garland.

Extra special thanks to the following:

Clare Christian, for providing self-publishing advice and continued belief when other book industry folk remained unconvinced. Graham Kibble-White, for unstinting moral support and proof-reading skills, over email, post, blog and phone. Richard Hollis and Lee Binding, for taking time to explain the intricacies of BBC Worldwide licensing. Tom Spilsbury and Peter Ware, of Doctor Who Magazine, for spreading the word to the fans. Gary Wales, for a typesetter's eye, and Jill Phythian, for Pantone help. Any of the errors in this book are nothing to do with them. Ian McArdell, for leading an excellent team of audio transcribers which also included Abby Peck, Laurie Hooper, David Whittam, Blake Connolly and Marie Parsons. Sue Armstrong and Miranda Mays, at Alzheimers Research UK, for ongoing assistance and encouragement. Marcus Gipps at Gollancz, for buying the first edition, and selling the second. Helen Ewing and Paul Hussey of Orion, who marshalled this new edition of the book through the complicated production process.

Lastly, thanks to Russell T Davies, for inspiration.

Alzheimer's Research UK

Alzheimer's Research UK is the UK's leading charity specialising in finding preventions, treatments and a cure for dementia. The charity relies entirely on donations to fund its vital research into Alzheimer's disease and other forms of dementia. To help defeat dementia, donate online today at www.alzheimersresearchuk.org or call 01223 843899.

Supporters

The publication of Behind the Sofa was only made possible by the generous support of the following sponsors, investors and donors.

Between them, they provided all the up-front funding required to pay for the book's design, illustration, layout, production and distribution.

Cairon Pearson

Company director, geek, Labradoodle lover
Was too scared to get close to the moving, talking Dalek at the Blackpool Doctor Who exhibition

Pre-VCR, as a child, I would revisit every adventure through its Target novelisation. Tom Baker would play as clearly in my imagination as he did on my TV. Several decades later I still watch, read and imagine what life would be like if I too were a Time Lord with a magic blue box...

Peter Shorney

Copywriter and wishful artist
Since childhood, has had problems saving money, thanks to Denys Fisher, Dapol, Character and Big Chief

Until 1979, my memory of TV was incoherent flashes. When I turned six, I watched *Destiny of the Daleks*. The now-familiar shapes burst onto the screen, terrifying Romana. I was right with her, scared and needing to know what happens next. I've wanted to know what happens next ever since...

Joel Baldwin

Estimator
Secretly wanted nothing more in life than the chance to build a police box in his backyard

My mum tells me I hid from the Daleks behind the settee. But I really fell in love with Doctor Who watching repeats during the 1980s where I live in Canada. Tom Baker was my favourite and stories like *The Stones of Blood* really captured my imagination. I have since travelled back home to England and visited Stonehenge hoping that, just maybe, I would see a cromlech move.

Steve Peachey

Half-hearted civil servant, whole-hearted Doctor Who fan
Was reduced to a tongue-tied seven-year-old in the combined presence of Tom Baker and Nicholas Courtney

Starting somewhere new can be a daunting experience, but it never ceases to amaze me how being a fan of Doctor Who helps. Many of my best and lasting friendships have come about in exactly that way. Folks, you know who you are, I thank you. And thank you too, Doctor — Doctors — for opening those doors!

Richard Starkings

Author of the comic book series, Elephantmen
Hid behind the sofa to watch Doctor Who, even at the risk of his brothers changing channels to Jimmy Clitheroe

My enduring memory of Doctor Who is, without doubt, the compassion, shock and outrage expressed by Jon Pertwee's Doctor when the Brigadier ordered the destruction of the Silurian base. I am now a practising Buddhist. In recent years, I have created the Exterminate font for comicbookfonts.com, and scripted the Tenth Doctor story, Cold-Blooded War, for IDW.

Dave Stevens

Groovy marketer into cutting-edge communications
*Made a dead realistic (honest!) mask of the Peking
Homunculus from a shoebox*

Doctor Who is one of my biggest passions and so I can't
fathom why my first memory is so low-key. It's of the Whomobile
taking to the air in *Planet of the Spiders*. Unconvincing effects
were lost on this four-year-old. It was amazing stuff! And I still think
Doctor Who is amazing stuff today.

Jordan M Royce

Editor of Starburst magazine since 2011
*Often played truant from school to visit the Blackpool
Doctor Who exhibition*

In a 1978 Issue of Starburst I discovered that there were two
Doctors before Jon Pertwee that I had never seen. With a BBC
repeat of *The Three Doctors* I finally encountered them in the flesh,
so to speak. It felt like I was meeting long lost relatives.

Investors

Darren Chandler
Melissa Dwyer
Richard Marklew
Sam Watts
Graham Kibble-White
Roger Clark
Stuart Wallace
Ruth Deller
Phillip Smith
Kevin Farrell
Shane Williams
Mark Oliver
Melissa Thorpe
Andy Harris
Sean Stokoe
Marie Parsons
John Bollan
Kenneth Duffy
Sean Cassity
Janet Skakle
Jonathan Hicks
Tony Rice
Andrew Cole
Ryan Evans
Simon Harries
Jack Lark
Christine Russell
Nigel Pennington
Jeffrey Root
Timothy Neal
Ulla-Maija Viitavuori
Jarrad Lee
James McFetridge
Barry Edwards

David Aldridge
Jack Kibble-White
Martyn Lesbirel
Steven Ricks
Richard Booker
Ross Garner
Peter Wilcock
Mark Phippen
Robert Berrow
Iain James Lawson
Rajesh Shah
Chris Overington
Neil Duffen
Fred Dillon
Stephen Miles
Christopher Bell
Ian Bridge
Stuart McCowan
Kevin Kairys
Andrew Statham
Matthew Hills
Steve Owen
Barry Patterson
Theresa McManus
Richard Meehan
Claire Hannon
Hywel McArdle
Kenneth Mason
Paul Levy
David Knill
Kathleen Jackson
Dave Robinson
Clive Cazeaux
Kristian Mears

Judith Jackson
Professor Joe Fenerty
Geraldine Fenerty
Richard Jones
Edward Hipkiss
Andrew Curran
Laura MacDonald
Darren Lake
Peter Brierley
Matthew Lebetkin
Vanessa Aisha Mostafa
Marc Hampson
Deborah Gannon
Joanne Biza
Liam Copsey
Andrew Kervell
Andrew Bell
Vitas Varnas

Anne Summerfield
David Pintar
Miss Hughes
Andrew Loretto
Simon Middleton
Joe McIntyre
Ewan Macleod
Gary Zielinski
Richard Atkins
David Adler
Sean Nicholas
Matthew Beckett
Ruth Bratt
Jessica Durkota
Clockhouse Studios
Dave Dixey
Mark Maddox

Donors

Vivienne Dunstan
Paul Jaunzems
Andy Piper
Bethany Moore
Jason Rhodes
Lewis Maddox
May Hane
Nick Mellish
Paul Dykes
Gavin Barrie
Mr P Greaves
David Rankin
David Mowbray
Vanessa Aisha Mostafa
Stephen Candy
Neil Coogan
Dan Hollingsworth

George Burden
Lexie Burden
Mathias Reeve
Jonathan Morris
Eddie Clements
Simon Hart
Nick Brown
Jason Smith
David Scott
Claire Rundell
Stephen Elsden
Chloe Allen
Dean Makin
Deborah Taylor
Robert Crawley
Andy Pontin
David Whittam

Lena Maher
Keith Lawrence
Leigh McAulay
Kenneth Plume
Anne Lane
Alan Wright
Catherine Kirk
Una McCormack
Glen Riordan
Dr Ash Smith
Martin Robinett
Michael Dennis
Hannah Cusworth
Simon Goodwin
Paul Goodison
Jo Evans
Eleanor Mackinnon
James Hewison-Carter
Barnaby Eaton-Jones
Arne Fischmann
Andy Phillips
David Brawn
Westley J Smith
Paul Norman
Paul Tayloe
Stephen Walters
Jon Deeming
Scott Pryde
Thomas Miller
Chris Orton
Craig Jordan
Uwe Sommerlad
Paula Painter
Carl Hellawell
Doug Gray
Michael Rees
Kate Taylor
Alan Clyde
Emrys Matthews
David Galan
Oliver Morris
Steven Manfred
Derek Vance
Randall Thomas

David T. Kirkpatrick
Alia Kirkpatrick
Yasmin Hailes
Jacqueline Smith
G P Russell
Andrew Scott
Mrs H Matthews
David Lewis
Rodney Hedrick
Page Turner Publishing
Danny Cartwright
Matthew Somerville
Jonathan Spencer
Antony Taylor
Katy Abram
Julian Knott
Kenneth Gray
Philip Browne
Laura Seymour
David Barsky
Ellie Warren
Kerry Frey
Steve Roberts
Sue Cowley
Michael Murray
Wayne Broughton
Melanie Broughton
Isaac Broughton
Graham Triggs
Sally Holmwood
John Williams
Gary Vernon
Christopher Ellis
Steve Duerden
Darren Allen
Alan Jones
Ed Salt
Nicholas Blake
Stuart Mitchell
Dallas Jones
Brian Kellett
Steve Morey
Frank Collins
Martin Bulmer

Mike Liddle
James McFetridge
Kevin Hoy
John Mooney
Richie Cheetham-Gerrard
Colleen Cheetham-Gerrard
Jon Spira
Barry Cooper
Matthew West
Phil Murray
Pierre L'Allier
John Hirst
Sean Brady
Carolanne Ybarra
John J Johnston
Ian Welch
LJ Warrick
Christopher Myers
Neil Micklewright
Lori B Witt
Sam Scott
TJ Worthington
Edward Allison
Jim Waller
Jason Brooks
David Shuttleworth
Nicholas Milton
Richard Oldfield
G Negus
Christopher Quy
Ben Haughton
Paul Engelberg
Christopher Leather
Mark Taylor
Steven Marsh
N J Fishwick
David Dovey
Daniel Slade
Gorman Christian
Helen Beeston
Edward Rackstraw
Nigel Adams
Blake Connolly
Christopher Morrison

Robert Turner
Rob Lannigan
Emily Frazer
Philip Davis
Laura Carr
Stewart Fearon
Dennis Orman
Ben Nielsen
Antony Thickitt
Stephen Pugh
Geraint Edwards
Bob Brinkman
Paul Andrew Brown
Eileene Coscolluela
Anthony Bliesner
Ian McLachlan
Stuart Feasey-Edwards
Julie Feasey-Edwards
Jack Kibble-White
Mr S C D Forster
Paal Forberg
James Wood
Ian Harris
David John Green
Colin Smith
Robert Getz
John Grace
Martin Geraghty
Will Jones
Richie J Haworth
Steven Walker
Mike Johnson
Geoff Whatmore
Richard Reeday
Alexander Hague
Kristian Ireland
Michael Wood
John-David Henshaw
Darryl Eddy
Ian Grice
Mark Smith
Briony Newbold
Karine Drexler
Paul Morris

About this book

Behind the Sofa is a collection of over 150 celebrity memories of Doctor Who, compiled in aid of Alzheimer's Research UK. The book has taken more than five years to put together and its publication was originally "crowd-funded" by the pre-orders of an enthusiastic Whovian community. Please get in touch and help spread the word online at www.doctorwhobook.com or on Twitter at @drwhobook.

Steve Berry is the author of TV Cream Toys and co-author of The Great British Tuck Shop. He has written for Doctor Who Magazine, Maxim and The Sun, among many other less-reputable periodicals. In 2003, he appeared alongside a Sontaran as a contributor to UK Gold's Doctor Who @ 40 weekend.

Ben Morris has provided monthly illustrations for Doctor Who Magazine since 2004, and works regularly for Doctor Who Adventures. His artwork has appeared in Radio Times, Daily Express, Daily Telegraph and the Brilliant Books of Doctor Who 2011 and 2012. He has also designed over 200 greetings cards.